research and report writing
for business and economics

research and report writing for business and economics

Conrad Berenson and Raymond R. Colton

both of The City University
of New York,
The Bernard M. Baruch College

Random House  New York

Library of Congress Catalog Card Number: 75-126896

Manufactured in the United States of America. Composed by Visual Skills, Inc., New York, N. Y. Printed and bound by Kingsport Press, Kingsport, Tenn.

First Edition

9876543

preface

This book is intended for those who are or expect to be engaged in business research or participate in day-to-day business operations and practices. The research and style principles offered here apply to the following fields of business and to economics: accounting, advertising, business forecasting, credit and collections, finance, foreign trade, industrial relations, insurance, business law, management, marketing, business mathematics, office management, purchasing, real estate, retailing, sales management, taxation, and traffic management.

Explanations in the text, though complete, are concise, to permit inclusion of illustrative materials and description of the many alternative approaches to specific research problems. "Style, in the technical sense here used is an accepted manner of dealing with certain forms of expression and details of typography. There are many styles; scholars, journals, presses and learned societies make them and change them."[1] Consequently, the authors of this book and their consultants screened available materials for pertinence, representativeness, usefulness, and, most important, conformity with accepted scholarly writing.

Writings from diverse fields—published in books, journals, pamphlets, and government publications—have been consulted. To their authors we are indebted, and throughout this book we have acknowledged specific contributions.

The authors have supervised undergraduate and graduate research studies for many years. Innumerable problems encountered in research work and preparation of the findings have been analyzed and their solutions illustrated here. This book is intended as a guide as much for the student who is writing his first paper as for the scholar who is preparing his doctoral dissertation.

The book is fairly comprehensive in its coverage of sources of business information; presentation of footnotes; selection of research topics; construction of tables, graphs, and illustrations; manuscript typing; and organization and outline systems. No book as brief as this one can, however, fully cover everything necessary to each researcher. Consequently, the authors have chosen to present Chapter 4, on research design and analysis, as an illustration, rather than

[1] William Riley Parker, *The MLA [Modern Language Association of America] Style Sheet* (New York: M.L.A., 1965), p. 3.

as a definitive examination, for this large subject calls for lengthy treatment beyond the scope of this book. At the same time they have included an extensive bibliography to this chapter, so that those who need additional information on research design can readily find it.

Conrad Berenson

May 1970   Raymond Colton

contents

list of figures

Figure

chapter 1
research in business and economics

The role of business and economics is central in our society, and their many aspects have therefore been subjected to a great deal of study. Some of this research is carried out in academic institutions, some in government and private agencies, and some in business firms. In all such studies, the data obtained must be recorded, analyzed, organized, and presented in a form that is useful. This book is devoted to setting forth the principles and techniques by which written work in business and economics can be presented.

What Business Is

"Business" is a very broad term that does not really suggest the many activities it subsumes. According to one widely read textbook, "Business is the sum total of all enterprises—agriculture, production, construction, distribution, transportation, communication, service establishments, and government—that play a part in the manufacture and marketing of goods and services to customers."[1] Another authoritative book declares that "man's desire to have certain goods and services made available to him and the efforts to supply and offer these goods and services for a consideration make up the concept of business."[2]

What Economics Is

The great economist Alfred Marshall wrote: "Economics is a study of men as they live and move and think in the ordinary business of life. But it concerns itself chiefly with those motives which affect, most powerfully and most steadily, man's conduct in the business part of his life."[3]

Kenneth Boulding, one of the nation's foremost economists, has commented that Marshall's definition is too broad. Boulding singles out three

[1] Vernon A. Musselman and Eugene H. Hughes, *Introduction to Modern Business: Analysis and Interpretation* (4th ed.; Englewood Cliffs, New Jersey: Prentice-Hall, Inc., 1964), p. 2.

[2] Michael J. Jucius and George R. Terry, *Introduction to Business* (3rd ed.; Homewood, Illinois: Richard D. Irwin, Inc., 1966), p. 3.

[3] Alfred Marshall, *Principles of Economics* (8th ed.; London, England: Macmillan and Co., Ltd., 1920), p. 14.

types of human activity that can be described as "economic": production, consumption, and exchange. He goes on to write that economics involves the *quantities* produced, consumed, and exchanged, as well as the *organizations* and *institutions* that direct economic activity.[4]

Economics and Business Compared

The definitions given here are fairly similar, for economics and business have much in common. In fact, in most universities the departments of business administration originated in the economics departments. Even today, many so-called "business" courses like consumer marketing and personnel management are taught in the department of economics. The training of those who major in one of the "business" disciplines—marketing, management, business statistics, accounting, and real estate, for example—strongly emphasizes economic study: the more advanced the training, the heavier the emphasis upon economics.

There *are* differences, however, between business administration and economics. Economics is the study primarily of the broader questions affecting the economic system: fiscal and monetary policy, business cycles, wage rates and levels, the banking system, and the like. Business administration and its constituent parts deal with more specific problems: marketing a product or product line, managing the labor force, accounting for the flow of funds into and out of the business, measuring the difference in effectiveness between two quality-control systems, and so on.

But any fine distinction between business and economics would be more arbitrary than real; the disciplines are far too interdependent and complementary for such an approach. The problems of "business" cannot be isolated from the problems of economics, and vice versa.[5]

The Study of Business

Any study of business and economics can be approached through one of several useful perspectives. The *functional* approach concentrates on those activities (or functions) common to a wide variety of industries, organizations, and products. Typical activities are buying, selling, advertising, credit management, warehousing, transportation, plant location, pricing, packaging, long-range planning, personnel management, legal supervision, accounting, quality control, and training. Each of these (and other) activities is carefully analyzed, and its relation to all other functions of the enterprise adjusted to optimize the long-range goals of that enterprise.[6]

The *institutional* approach is based on categories that have been developed to classify the nation's business activity, for example, manufacturing

[4]Kenneth Boulding, *Economic Analysis* (3rd ed.; New York: Harper & Brothers, 1955), pp. 3-4.
[5]Rollin H. Symonds, Richard E. Ball, and Eugene J. Kelley, *Business Administration: Problems and Functions* (Boston: Allyn and Bacon, Inc., 1962), pp. 6-7.
[6]Jucius and Terry, *op. cit.*, pp. 114-119.

enterprises, wholesalers, retail enterprises, raw-materials suppliers, credit-creating agencies (banks), and credit-regulating agencies (governments). For each *institutional category,* we seek to identify characteristic parameters, methods of operation, attributes, needs, and so on.

There is also an *industry* or *commodity* approach, which focuses on all the characteristics, needs, opportunities, environments, and so on, related to a particular industry or commodity. Thus, we might study the chemical industry, the steel industry, or the television industry; we might examine such products as wheat, benzene, sulfuric acid, telephones, and breakfast cereals.[7,8]

Economists view the array of issues, policies, and activities with which they must cope from two primary perspectives—*microeconomic* and *macroeconomic. Microeconomics* is the study of individual firms, households, prices, incomes, industries, and commodities; it puts each under a microscope, as it were. The most relevant economic tools are supply-and-demand analysis, marginal analysis, and the like.[9,10] *Macroeconomics* is the study of the *whole* economy; it deals with aggregates, rather than with the particular elements that constitute the system. A study of the pricing of sulfuric acid or of acids in general falls within the scope of microeconomics, of the price level of the economy as a whole within that of macroeconomics.

Whatever view is taken, the American business and economic system is predominantly characterized by free-enterprise capitalism, not however, laissez-faire capitalism but a form in which the government takes an active role to preserve a balance between what is good for the individual citizen and what is good for the business firm.[11]

Characteristics of American Business

At this point it is logical to introduce some characteristics of American business, to orient the reader to the system he will be studying.

Today American Gross National Product is nearing the $1,000 billion level and is increasing by about 4 percent each year. The businesses contributing to this tremendous quantity of goods and services range from the American Telephone & Telegraph Company, with its $25 billion in assets, to individuals operating "out of their hats." It is an economic system characterized by change, by an increasingly high level of technology, by mass production and mass consumption, and by steadily increasing capital investment in each worker. The range of capital investment, for example, runs from about $4,000 per worker in

[7]See, for example, the *industry study:* Conrad Berenson, et al., *Administration of the Chemical Enterprise* (New York: John Wiley & Sons, Inc., 1963).

[8]See also, the *product study, Isopropyl Alcohol* (New York: Enjay Chemical Co., 1966).

[9]Lawrence Abbott, *Economics and the Modern World* (New York: Harcourt, Brace and Co., 1960), pp. 213, 454.

[10]Boulding, *op. cit.,* p. 237.

[11]Alfred Kuhn, *The Study of Society* (Homewood, Illinois: Richard D. Irwin, Inc., 1963), pp. 541-555.

the apparel industry to $103,000 per worker in the petroleum industry.[12] Such huge investments are, of course, repaid in high productivity of the industries in which they are made. Today the average worker produces about six times the output of his counterpart a century ago.[13] We have every reason to expect that productivity will continue to increase; in fact, raising the national standard of living depends upon such an increase.

Trends and Problems in American Business

The complexity of the vast business system sketched in the preceding section, together with its dynamism, technical change, and so on, present many problems and, concomitantly, many opportunities for those who can solve problems. Research to define these problems and opportunities and to develop solutions for them is of vital importance to our society, which is a *business* society; any major business issue or opportunity therefore ipso facto warrants the most intelligent and well-reasoned investigation by the most talented individuals in our business culture.

What are some of these business problems? What opportunities do they engender? Here we shall introduce in broad fashion some of today's major trends and issues.

Mergers and Acquisitions. The number of corporate combinations of all kinds is increasing rapidly and was estimated at more than 2,000 in 1966.[14] Many problems arise from this trend, for example, potential reciprocity in buying and selling, concentration of industry, price controls, plant dislocation, personnel changes, higher entry costs for new products, and so on.

The Influence of Organized Labor. Although the size of labor-union membership is relatively static, its economic power is not. The power to wreak severe economic damage on the business community and society as a whole is great and the danger of its abuse very real. The next few years promise many disagreements between management and labor, in which such abuse of this great power will have to be carefully avoided.

The Utilization of R&D Results. In 1969 the nation's bill for research and development was about $26 billion.[15] Unfortunately, a very significant share of this massive investment is not converted into useful products within our

---

[12]Theodore J. Sielaff and John W. Aberle, *Introduction to Business: American Enterprise in Action* (2nd ed.; Belmont, California: Wadsworth Publishing Co., Inc., 1966), pp. 5-20.

[13]Musselman and Hughes, *op. cit.,* p. 35.

[14]"Will the Government Challenge Your Merger?", *Business Management* (November, 1966), Vol. 31, No. 2, pp. 58-72.

[15]Victor J. Danilov, "$26 Billion for Research", *Industrial Research* (January, 1969), Vol. 11, No. 1, pp. 62-66.

economic system. Some reasons why are known; others are not. In any event, successful conversion of this investment into increased GNP and a higher standard of living is one of the most vital challenges facing our economic system, especially as this system is fed and nourished by innovation and technological advance.

Long-Range Planning. Only in the last several years has long-range planning become a recognized function of the modern business enterprise. Because it is so new, many firms are having difficulties in successfully implementing it.[16] Yet the function is now so important that these difficulties must be overcome if the firms' long-range profits and survival prospects are to be maximized.

Many more key areas could be cited and extensive works written about each; among them are changes in business ethics and social attitudes, development of econometric models, reduction of tariff barriers among nations, relations between government and labor, effects of automation, reduced demand for unskilled labor, and the changing relations between manufacturing and service industries.

The Need for Research

Research is the basis on which business firms and society analyze existing situations and initiate change. The success of the economic system depends upon the ability of its members to conduct that research satisfactorily.[17]

Fortunately, there has been emphasis not only upon product and technological research (which accounted for expenditures of $24 billion in 1967) but also upon business and economic research. It has been estimated, for example, that in marketing research alone, expenditures have grown from $24 million in 1940 to $100 million in 1950 to $300 million in 1960, to $425 million in 1965, and to more than $700 million in 1970. In fact, in recent years marketing-research expenditures have grown about twice as fast as GNP.[18] Economic researchers are also in great demand, and at present there is a considerable shortage of good research economists. Business and government organizations are being structured to depend more and more heavily upon their research staffs for guidance in all their planning programs.

Universities have recognized this increased emphasis upon research, and

[16]E. Kirby Warren, *Long-Range Planning: The Executive Viewpoint* (Englewood Cliffs, New Jersey: Prentice-Hall, Inc., 1966), *passim.*

[17]Robert Ferber and P. J. Verdoorn, *Research Methods in Economics and Business* (New York: The Macmillan Co., 1962), pp. 3, 7.

[18]Albert Blankenship and Joseph B. Doyle, *Marketing Research Management* (New York: American Management Association, 1965), pp. 12-15.

for degrees in business and economics many of them now require research reports from their students. On the undergraduate level this requirement includes specific course papers and, for honors courses and seminars, usually longer research reports nearly equivalent to master's theses. Master's programs in business and economics often require formal theses, as well as research papers of various lengths and levels of sophistication in other courses. On the doctoral level, each student must write a dissertation that demonstrates a high level of competence in the investigation of a problem; in addition, he too must satisfy the usual course requirements for term papers and reports.

Hypotheses

Most research requires a *hypothesis* as a basis. Hypotheses are "provisional or temporary theories—held only until all the evidence has been collected and one of the possible solutions has been decided upon as the correct one...."[19] A hypothesis serves two principal purposes: to direct the thinking and investigations of the researcher and to suggest the best research methods for attacking the particular problem.[20] It is thus a "working assumption," or position, from which the research effort is launched. It is not an immutable rock upon which the researcher's work *must forevermore be based* and which is used to cast shadows on or bury the facts as they are uncovered.

A satisfactory hypothesis should explain facts that have not previously been adequately explained, be consistent with all known facts, be as simple as possible while still accounting for all relevant data, aid in prediction of events and relations, be susceptible to verification or refutation, and indicate the most appropriate research methods for attacking the problem.

At this point, we must ask "How then is this working premise or hypothesis to be formulated?" It is developed during the process of exploring the nature of the problem which is under investigation. Generally, working hypotheses arise from assessment of the data which one uncovers by searching the literature, by interviewing experts in the subject area, by looking for relationships in the data and reasoning inductively, by preliminary field trials, by discussing the problem with associates, by drawing analogies from similar problems in other fields, and so on.

When the researcher adopts his preliminary, or working, hypothesis, he then gears his efforts to test it—that is, to collect facts that will enable him to accept, modify, or reject it. If, upon analysis, the data do support the hypothesis, then he need not search for another; if they do *not* support it, he must reexamine all the data and formulate another working hypothesis. Chapter 4 demonstrates *how* the data that have been gathered can be analyzed.

Some problems do not require any hypothesis; they mainly require determination of the facts but no analysis of them. Preparation of a list of all the

[19] Tyrus Hillway, *Introduction to Research* (2nd ed.; Boston: Houghton Mifflin Co., 1964), p. 122.

[20] Ferber and Verdoorn, *op. cit.*, pp. 35-37.

producers of nitric acid in the world classified by manufacturing method would require no hypothesis; it would simply be a job of fact finding. But if the researcher wishes to draw conclusions about why certain processes of manufacturing nitric acid are more frequently used than are others and to generalize his conclusions, he needs a hypothesis.

A sample hypothesis can be constructed from the following situation. Assume that you are going to do research on a major problem in marketing: the product life cycle. Your first step will be to read all that you can about these cycles (which will not be very much) and to talk to a few experienced and talented marketing professionals. Assume further that, when you analyze the results of this search, you note that the literature has failed to cover a crucial phase in a product's life—the abandonment phase. You then search the literature on abandonment fairly freely, seeking some insight into this phase. As a result of this reading and additional conversations with professionals, colleagues, and so on, you then decide that you can make a definite contribution by thoroughly studying the abandonment phase of the product life cycle. You believe that you can organize the facts about abandonment in a useful framework, or model. Hence, you postulate, as your hypothesis, the following:

"The hypothesis that will be investigated in this paper is that a product-abandonment model can be constructed to guide the firm to the 'right' product-abandonment decision. This model will be an analogue and will tie together, in a concise and compatible framework, the significant variables that bear upon the abandonment decisions."

Planning and Organizing the Research

Good results in business and economic research depend upon careful planning and organization. Half the chapters in this book have been devoted to these elements. The first step is the selection of a general subject area (see Chapter 2).[21] Then the researcher must study the historical background of his problem thoroughly and must acquaint himself with all of the significant facts related to it; this part of the research job is explored in Chapter 3, on sources of information.

Once the subject has been selected and some background information gathered the student must develop his hypothesis and define the scope of his work (see Chapter 17, "Coordinating Content").

It is important to note that these stages of planning and organization are not simply sequential; they must be continually repeated until the researcher has really pinpointed his task and approach. In fact, the sequence itself must often be altered. For example, although it is logically true that the first step is to select the topic, practically one may begin with a random search through the literature simply to obtain ideas. The initially selected *subject area* is then narrowed to a *topic* suitable for a research project. Then a hypothesis must be

[21] J. Francis Rummel and Wesley C. Ballaine, *Research Methodology in Business* (New York: Harper & Row, 1963), pp. 43-44.

framed from this topic and the literature and other sources searched *again* to determine whether or not the hypothesis is viable. Once the hypothesis seems fairly well established, the search must be resumed along more specific lines suggested by the scope and limits of the project.

During these activities the researcher may also be taking notes (Chapter 5), conducting interviews (Chapter 6), planning and distributing questionnaires (Chapter 7), perhaps already beginning to organize his material according to one or more clearly specified plans (Chapter 8); the working outline for the final manuscript is developed as the information is collected and organized for analysis (Chapter 9).

Reporting the Research Results

The other half of the chapters in this book are designed to familiarize the student with the commonly accepted forms for presenting his research results. There are chapters on footnotes, tables, graphs and illustrations, quotations, use of numbers, style, typing, editing, and putting the various parts together.

The user of this book will gain from selectivity in using its contents. A student writing a course report can skim through some chapters, for example, that on questionnaires, but should read others, like Chapter 3, on sources of information, more carefully. If this topic is assigned by the instructor—as it often is for a term paper—then Chapter 2 can be omitted.

Students writing theses or dissertations will use more of the manual, but they can still be selective; if their work requires neither interviews nor questionnaires, for example, the two relevant chapters can be omitted.

The usefulness of the different chapters of this book depends also upon the *nature* of the research task; does it involve an experiment, fact finding, or a critical interpretation? Brief examples of each of these research categories will serve to illustrate the types.

Experiment. In an experiment controlled conditions are established so that the hypothesis can be examined. A study of the effectiveness of a new job-induction program might require its introduction in one division of a company while the traditional programs were continued in the other divisions. Then a correlation between the nature of the job-induction program and the rate of labor turnover in each division could be sought.

Fact Finding. Fact finding involves no attempt to generalize from the facts or to use them to solve a problem.[22] For example, one may trace the price of gold in the United States since George Washington was inaugurated, compile a bibliography of all books on mergers and acquisitions published in the United States since 1900, or measure sales of a breakfast cereal in supermarkets in New England during a certain month.

---

[22] Hillway, *op. cit.*, pp. 99-101.

Critical Interpretation. In interpretive research there is heavy emphasis upon the *judgments* of the researcher. Of course, these judgments must be based on logic and supported by the data. This approach thus builds upon fact finding, but, unlike the latter, attempts to solve problems and to make generalizations or recommendations. An example would be a study of mergers and acquisitions in manufacturing companies in which facts about why these firms decided to combine were uncovered. Then, the researcher would analyze the facts and perhaps draw conclusions about why manufacturing firms in general might find combining advisable. Indeed, the researcher might even be able to predict which organizations would engage in some form of corporate combination.

In studying why firms combine, however, it is possible that conclusions can be drawn only in relation to the organizations in the sample. It simply might not be possible to extend the conclusions beyond this point; inferences and hypotheses could perhaps be made but not generalizations to any larger universe.

On the other hand, the researcher might explore a field in order later to formulate and test a theory that could explain and predict certain behavior. Although insights could be gained from such a study, they might not necessarily be conclusions in a rigorous sense but simply indications that a particular approach to the development of a general theory might warrant additional investigation and would therefore be worth reporting in this preliminary form.

This book cannot make diligent research, ingenious experiments, and careful analysis unnecessary. Rather it is designed to facilitate these activities and to assist you to the successful conclusion of your written work by guiding you logically through the steps necessary to a good final manuscript.

Bibliography

Abbott, Lawrence, *Economics and the Modern World* (New York: Harcourt, Brace and Co., 1960), pp. xiv + 880.

Blankenship, Albert, and Joseph B. Doyle, *Marketing Research Management* (New York: American Management Association, 1965), pp. viii + 370.

Boulding, Kenneth, *Economic Analysis* (3rd ed.; New York: Harper & Brothers, 1955), pp. xx + 905.

Ferber, Robert, and P. J. Verdoorn, *Research Methods in Economics and Business* (New York: The Macmillan Co., 1962), pp. xiv + 573.

Hillway, Tyrus, *Introduction to Research* (2nd ed.; Boston: Houghton Mifflin Co., 1964), pp. xi + 308.

Jucius, Michael J., and George R. Terry, *Introduction to Business* (3rd ed.; Homewood, Illinois: Richard D. Irwin, Inc., 1966), pp. xii + 564.

Kuhn, Alfred, *The Study of Society* (Homewood, Illinois: Richard D. Irwin, Inc., 1963), pp. xviii + 810.

Musselman, Vernon A., and Eugene H. Hughes, *Introduction to Modern Business: Analysis and Interpretation* (4th ed.; Englewood Cliffs, New Jersey: Prentice-Hall, Inc., 1964), pp. xiv + 658.

Rummel, J. Francis, and Wesley C. Ballaine, *Research Methodology in Business* (New York: Harper & Row, 1963), pp. xvi + 359.

Sielaff, Theodore J., and John W. Aberle, *Introduction to Business: American Enterprise in Action* (2nd ed.; Belmont, California: Wadsworth Publishing Co., Inc., 1966), pp. xiii + 623.

Symonds, Rollin H., Richard E. Ball, and Eugene J. Kelley, *Business Administration: Problems and Functions* (Boston: Allyn and Bacon, Inc., 1962), pp. xx + 535.

Tarshis, Lorie, *Modern Economics: An Introduction* (Boston: Houghton Mifflin Co., 1967), pp. 795.

Warren, E. Kirby, *Long-Range Planning: The Executive Viewpoint* (Englewood Cliffs, New Jersey: Prentice-Hall, Inc., 1966), pp. xvi + 108.

chapter 2
selecting a topic

Topics for reports are often assigned by the instructor; for theses and dissertations the students' selection of suitable topics is the most crucial aspect of the entire work. Without a good topic, you will founder in a morass of difficulties. A poorly chosen and ill-defined topic seldom results in a good manuscript.

This section of the book provides you with guidelines for the selection of a topic that will permit you to write the best manuscript possible. Since the problems of selecting a topic for a graduate thesis or dissertation are more stringent than for a term paper, the former will be emphasized in the discussion below. This will permit those students who are given term paper assignments to benefit from the more extensive guidelines used for theses and dissertations.

What Makes a Good Topic

As most students have written few reports and no thesis or dissertation before they begin that assignment for their degree, the reader should be neither surprised nor embarrassed if he does not know what constitutes a suitable topic. A few guidelines will be helpful here.

First, a topic should not be *simply* a summary or a review of what authorities say. If their works can be analyzed, interpreted to elucidate a point of view, or recombined to present new insights, however, then the *analytical* nature of the effort may make the subject acceptable for a master's degree or a term paper. A dissertation is expected to contribute to knowledge, and primary research is essential.

Second, it should not be *simply* a narration of your experiences and opinions, as though you were an expert.[1] The researcher's unsupported opinions are not acceptable; a thesis or report requires research and direct reference to authorities in support of its assertions.

Third, it should not be a study of a problem unique to a single

---

[1]Occasionally, the author of a manuscript is already a widely recognized expert in his profession or occupation. He is qualified to report his personal observations of that area in which he *is* an authority.

organization, although a single firm can be used to illustrate a problem common to many.

Your study must be an attempt to solve a problem or test a hypothesis; it must present, interpret, and cogently defend a point of view based upon research and analysis of the data; it must either offer new and useful knowledge or collate and analyze information from scattered sources in new and more useful form. Your manuscript should reflect your careful examination of the relevant literature, that is, secondary research; careful primary research, for example, through a field questionnaire or laboratory investigation; or both.

A good general guide to help you determine whether or not you are selecting a good topic is to ask yourself and some of your fellow students, "Will this be *useful* work?" The key resides in its *utility,* for example, a mere summary is seldom useful, but a well-organized critical analysis can be very useful. Remember that additions to or modifications of a theory can be useful too, both to the academician and to the businessman. Finally, another guide that will help you decide is to weigh whether you are being a reporter or an analyst; the former is usually not enough for a thesis or report—with the exception of those times when the utility would be extremely high—but, the latter usually provides a good and entirely acceptable basis for your effort.

A dissertation topic conforms to these principles, except that it must be concerned above all with primary research "in depth" and must avoid duplication of similar efforts. Analytical work is preferable to purely descriptive work, and a theoretical framework permitting the use of quantitative analytical techniques—for example, comparison of one group of variables to another—should be established.

Carving a Topic Out of the Subject

One of the most difficult research tasks is to carve out a suitable portion of a subject area as a subarea, or *topic,* for the thesis or dissertation. A *subject* is a broad area of study; a *topic* is the part of that area selected for your paper.

The primary source of failure to produce an acceptable report or thesis is in *defining* the problem properly. Do not set initial limits that are too broad; experience has proved that, once research begins, new avenues open up and necessitate further limitation of the topic. It is far better to choose a narrow phase of your topic than to be too general, for it is much easier to broaden the scope of your work later, if necessary, than to narrow it. There are several factors to consider in the initial narrowing of a subject area to a manageable topic. The following instructions are seemingly written for a thesis or dissertation but often apply to term papers too.

Seek the Advice of Your Instructor. Your instructor can help you to select a general subject. It is not his job to tell you what topic to write on, but he can guide you to the point at which you are able to select it. (If your adviser selected the topic for you he would deprive you of a skill that you *must* have for survival in the business world.) To make the most of this source of advice, choose your instructor according to your own interests and his specialities, as far as your school permits. Ask him to recommend three good theses (or dissertations) completed by his students in recent years; reading them will give you an idea of what he and the school expect. Be sure to obtain the instructor's *written* approval of your topic before you proceed.

Examine Your Ability to Perform. Are the subject and topic in an area in which you have studied widely? If you are planning to write on mergers and acquisitions, for example, be sure that you know enough about corporate finance to do the job well. Do you also have sufficient interdisciplinary knowledge to do the job? For example, a study of the automobile market requires enough statistical knowledge to analyze the data. If you lack sufficient knowledge of the primary field and its related disciplines, can you obtain it within a reasonable time? Can you afford the expense of writing this paper, thesis, or dissertation? There may be questionnaires to print, mail, and tabulate; travel and computer expenses may be substantial. What is your estimate of the probability of success in writing a good manuscript? of failure?

The Availability of Data. Do you have the time to do the job? If you want to take your degree in one year, do not propose, for example, an experimental study of the long-run effects of innovations in management-training programs; such a study, to obtain truly long-run data, must continue well beyond one year. Will you have to travel to obtain the data you need? What are the possibilities of delay in obtaining your data? Will you have to prepare a questionnaire, mail it, and wait for replies? What are the penalties of delay in conducting the research? Will interview respondents move? Will conditions in your subject field change?

Are sufficient data available at all? A good rule of thumb for writing a thesis in the area of business is to average at least one reference per page (there are many exceptions to this rule, especially in original work); the entire thesis may be 60-125 pages. For a dissertation two or three references per page are common. The usual length of a dissertation in management, marketing, finance, and accounting is 170-300 pages or more. A good term paper can be only 10-15 pages.

The Novelty of the Topic. Has the topic been treated before? often? recently? If it has previously been treated will your adviser approve an up-to-date study? Will he approve a new approach or a more detailed investigation? Are there sufficient new data to justify an additional thesis on the topic?

The Importance of the Topic. Is the topic of interest to you, to your university, to the community, to Federal or state government agencies, to your employer, to trade associations, to philanthropic institutions, and so on? Can the topic for a master's thesis be expanded to a doctoral dissertation by you? Can a term paper provide the basis for a master's thesis? What is the publication potential of this topic?

Avoiding the "Magnum-Opus Syndrome." Your manuscript is not expected to represent your life's work; do not behave as if it were. If you envision the study as an enormous task, your anxiety may drive you to collect many more data than you need. The manuscript is intended only as a formal exercise in research, analysis, and writing and at the doctoral level as a modest contribution to knowledge. It should be of moderate scope.

Seeking the Right Focus. In defining your topic consider that a number of variables are involved in any situation. It does not matter at first whether or not you recognize which are dependent and independent. It *is* important that you recognize the possibility of impact of one variable upon another, for example, of price changes upon sales volume or of job-induction techniques upon workers' morale. You must also recognize that other variables can affect the situation on which you are focusing: sales volume can also be influenced by advertising, promotion, packaging, and so on, whereas morale can be influenced not only by job-induction techniques but also by salaries, nature of the job, location of the firm, and so on. Once you recognize the need to concentrate upon one or a few variables, then you can more readily select those within a certain problem area for your investigation.

Example of Selecting a Topic: Management

Let us begin by assuming that you are matriculated for a master's or doctoral degree in management. The time has come to register for the thesis or dissertation course and to select an appropriate topic.

As your field is management, you must write your paper on some aspect of management and not on marketing, statistics, or some other field. One way to begin is to go to the library and screen the *Business Periodicals Index* for ideas. In addition, you should examine the tables of contents in recent issues of journals that publish articles on management, for example, *Harvard Business Review, Administrative Science Quarterly, Journal of the Academy of Management, Management Science, Nation's Business, Industrial Research, Fortune, Business Management, Business Horizons,* and the *California Management Review.* A survey of reference works in various business fields is presented in Chapter 3.

After browsing among these sources, you may find, for example, that employee turnover is a subject of considerable current interest and importance. Of course, employee turnover is far too broad for your topic, but after additional library work you may conclude that one of its subareas, job induction, is not.

Next, you formulate a subject area in terms that reveal whether or not treatment can be both analytical and useful, for example, "A Critical Evaluation of Job-Induction Techniques."

At this point, your instructor may point out that, although the subject is indeed useful, it is still far too broad; you still have not developed a viable topic from the general subject.

Now you refer to our section on carving a topic out of the subject for guidance in setting limits. Your preliminary research has shown that job induction is ordinarily divided into seven key phases (see Figure 1) and you therefore decide to limit your work to just the phase of rotation of work assignments.

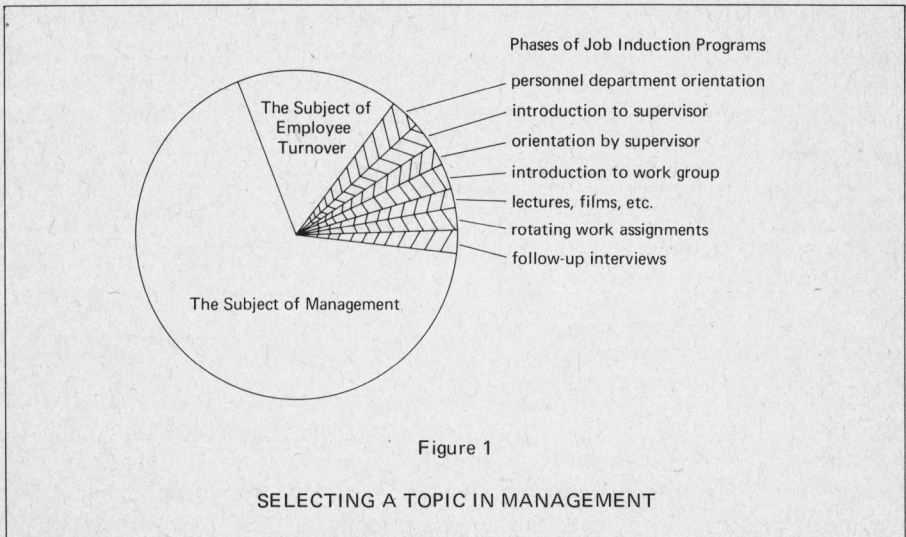

Phases of Job Induction Programs

personnel department orientation

introduction to supervisor

orientation by supervisor

introduction to work group

lectures, films, etc.

rotating work assignments

follow-up interviews

The Subject of
Employee
Turnover

The Subject of Management

Figure 1

SELECTING A TOPIC IN MANAGEMENT

But will "An Examination of the Rotating Work Assignment Phase of Recent Job-Induction Programs" be suitable? Again you review the questions on carving out a topic; you may find that it is still too broad. You can narrow it further to "The Effects of Rotating Work Assignments on Turnover Rates of Young Engineers." A final review of the acceptance criteria suggests a high probability of success with this limited topic. You secure the written approval of your instructor, and you are ready to write the prospectus.

Example of Selecting a Topic: Marketing

Let us take another example of topic selection, this time from the field of marketing. Assume that you are employed in the technical end of the chemical industry and have been taking courses toward an M.B.A. degree; you have become interested in marketing research. Logically enough, you decide to write your thesis on a topic that deals with both the chemical industry and market research.

Your first step is to examine the key indexes (see Chapter 3) for such a combined subject area. These indexes will include the *Business Periodicals Index* and the *Applied Science and Technology Index.* You search under a number of categories for ideas that will perhaps lead to an acceptable topic.

It is necessary to search the indexes under various headings and sub-headings for two primary reasons. First, casting a broad net is more likely to result in ideas. Second, you can never be sure under what heading articles on a combination like the chemical industry and market research will be indexed. You therefore look under such headings as "Chemicals," "Chemical Industry," "Industry," "Industrial Marketing," "Industrial Chemicals," "Chemical Market Research," "Market Research," "Market Research—Chemicals," and so on.

As it usually takes a few months before journal articles are indexed, you also study the tables of contents in recent issues of journals relevant to your interest, for example, *Journal of Marketing, Journal of Marketing Research, Journal of Advertising Research, Commentary, Harvard Business Review, California Management Review, Business Horizons, Sales Management, Industrial Marketing, Management Science, Printers' Ink, Journal of Business, Chemical Week, Chemical & Engineering News, Chemical Purchasing,* and *Chemical Engineering.*

In examining the indexes and tables of contents and reading some of the more intriguing articles, you may notice, first, a good deal of activity in the field of test marketing and much apparent disagreement over its value.[2,3] Many articles have recently been published on this subject, and you think that you may be able to tie them together in some way—perhaps by setting in a clear and useful perspective the arguments of each of the several schools of thought about test marketing and then determining which offers the most valid approach. After examining the literature on the chemical industry and familiarizing yourself with the industry's problems, however, you conclude that, because of its special marketing approach, test marketing is not a good idea.[4]

You review the sources again, and you realize that arguments on the value of test marketing may be symptomatic of a general lack of knowledge about the value of market research itself! You then redirect your search to see just what has been written on this subject. You find amazingly little of a substantial nature; many people have written that market research is worthwhile, but few have tried to establish guidelines for measuring its value and conducting the firm's market research programs based on sound principles rather than on only hope and enthusiasm. One article by Ralph L. Day says, "The literature of marketing research is quite extensive with regard to methods of conducting and analyzing research but is practically non-existent with regard to determining how much research a firm should do or how to choose among alternative projects."[5]

This statement interests you, and you think there may be an opportunity to write about some aspect of the problem stated by Day. His criticism

---

[2] Jack A. Gold, "Testing Test Market Predictions", *Journal of Marketing Research* (August, 1964), Vol. 1, No. 3, pp. 41-53.

[3] "Test Marketing: Solid Sales Tool or Waste of Money?", *Sales Management* (Dec. 1, 1966), Vol. 97, No. 13, pp. 41-45, 68.

[4] Conrad Berenson, *Administration of the Chemical Enterprise* (New York: John Wiley & Sons, Inc., 1963), pp. 1-43.

[5] Ralph L. Day, "Optimizing Market Research Through Cost-Benefit Analysis", *Business Horizons* (Fall, 1966), Vol. 9, No. 3, p. 49.

Interest in Market Research   Employment in the
                                               Chemical Industry

review of indexes, tables of contents

reading of key articles

Formulation of First Subject Area:
"The Value of Test Marketing"

Rejection of First Subject

review of indexes, tables of contents, and
key articles

Formulation of Second Subject Area:
"What is the Value of Market Research?"

refinement of Second Subject Area to:
"How to Evaluate Market-Research Results"

further refinement of Second Subject Area to:
"How Chemical Companies Evaluate Market-
Research Results"

consultation with your instructor and
narrowing latter refinement to:
"The Use of Budgetary Control by Market-
Research Departments of Chemical Firms"

instructor's approval of latter topic

begin work on thesis prospectus

Figure 2

**FLOW CHART FOR THE GENERATION OF A
THESIS TOPIC**

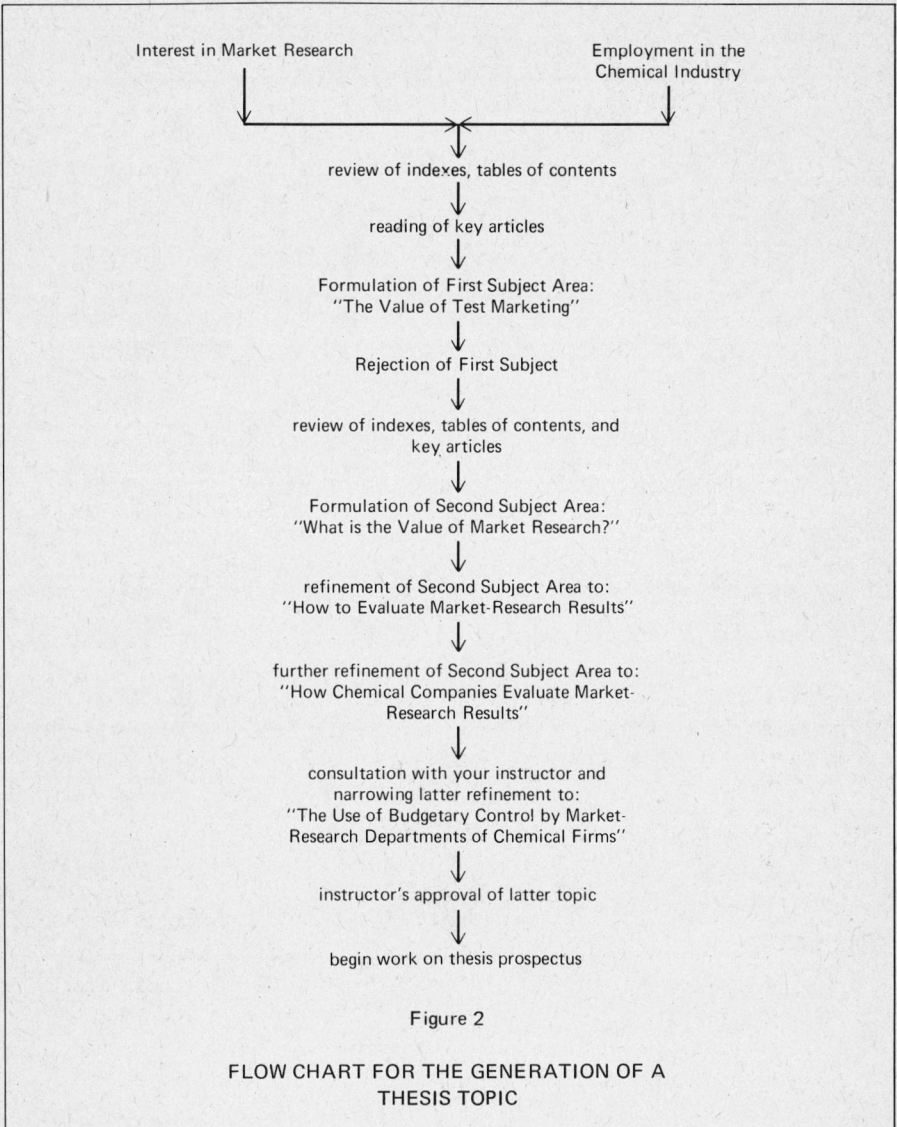

really applies to the area of managerial evaluation and control of market research. Once again you examine the sources and find that very little has been written about evaluating market-research programs. You thus formulate your subject as "How to Evaluate Market-Research Results." But you realize that this subject is pretty big, and you also have an interest in the chemical industry. You narrow the topic to "How Chemical Companies Evaluate Market-Research Results."

You consult your instructor, and he convinces you that the topic is still too broad, although the subject is extremely important. Now you limit your project still further to investigation of how chemical firms use just one managerial technique, the budget, to control their market-research activities. You state your topic: "The Use of Budgetary Control by Market-Research Departments of Chemical Firms."

Your instructor approves the topic, and you set to work on your prospectus.

Figure 2 outlines the steps you took to get to this point.

chapter 3
sources of information
on business

The purpose of this chapter is to survey the *major* literature resources available to the student writing a report, thesis, or dissertation in the field of business. Careful, persistent, and imaginative use of these resources can contribute to thorough exploration of many business problems. The bibliography at the end of this chapter provides additional guides to available sources.

Sources of Data

Books. The first place to look for information on an unfamiliar topic is in an appropriate book that will provide enough basic information to give you an overview of the subject. Once such a perspective has been obtained, you can turn to more specialized books and to periodicals.

The easiest and most efficient way to find books on your topic is to refer to the card catalogue in your library. On the card for each book the subject heading, title, author's name, publisher, publication date, call numbers, number of pages, cross-reference headings, and sometimes a note on the contents are printed. Usually every book in the library is listed on three separate cards, which are filed alphabetically under the author's name, the title, and the subject.

In using the subject cards, try to find the narrowest appropriate segment of your subject that is indexed. Screening *all* books listed under "Management," for example, would be quite a chore, but, if your topic is "production control," it is fairly easy to examine each book in the subcategory "Management—Controls."

Sometimes no book can be found on your specific subject area. It is then essential to consult books on related areas. They may provide valuable material. Your library may not have a single book on production control, but it may have many on production engineering or production management, and they may have chapters on production control.

Using a basic book index is similar to using the card catalogue. *The Cumulative Book Index: A World List of Books in the English Language* is a valuable tool for all researchers. It lists by author, title, and subject all books published in English in any country and is issued monthly, except for August.

Articles. Business conditions change far too rapidly for books to be of primary value to most students of current business. It takes many months and generally several years for secondary materials (articles, papers, and so on) to be collected, collated, and integrated in a book—a lapse that you can avoid by using articles, public documents, and monographs and the like as much as you can in preference to books.

The problem of how to find journal articles that will be relevant remains, however. It is not as difficult as it may seem at first, despite the enormous number of periodicals published. Many articles dealing with business are indexed in several widely available indexes; in fact, most highly respected sources of information on business are *always* indexed in these sources.

A few minutes spent thumbing through one of the indexes listed in this chapter will give you a good idea of what to expect from them. The key to using a subject index successfully is to remember that, although information is filed according to topic, the subject itself can be described under a number of different headings. Imagination in making a checklist of relevant headings is a critical step in finding the periodical references you need. Reference should be made to a dictionary or thesaurus for synonymous terms describing key topics to be treated in your work.

The importance of seeking entries under as many different headings as possible can be briefly illustrated. Assume that your subject is the process of introducing new compensation plans to the work force and that your tentative topic is "techniques in introducing new wage plans." Relevant periodical references may be found under such index headings as "Wages," "Salaries," "Compensation," "Earnings," "Production—Wage Costs," "Costs—Production Workers" "Costs—Salary," "Product Costs—Earnings," "Payroll," "Production—Wages," "Workers—Income," "Payments—Salaries," "Payments—Factory Workers." In fact, it is quite common for a checklist of categories to contain twenty or thirty entries.

Ordinarily, it is wise to comb entries under each heading over a ten-year period, starting with the latest volume of the index and working back. A word of caution, however: if your topic involves continual significant developments, you must be careful not to rely too much on an article that is old; for example, an article on electronic data processing that is more than five years old will not have accurate information on the current situation.

An economic-geography textbook or an atlas published before 1959 is necessarily outdated. For example, from 1959 to 1967, thirty-four new countries were created, fifteen changed their names, thirty-two changed their international boundaries, and fifty-eight changed their internal boundaries.

Once you have a good checklist of subject headings, the next step is to know which indexes are most useful.

For business research the most important is the *Business Periodicals Index*. One hundred sixty-eight business journals are indexed in each of eleven issues a year; the issues are cumulatively indexed three times a year and annually.[1]

[1] A.J. Walford (ed.), *Guide to Reference Material, Supplement* (London, England: The Library Association, 1963), p. 180.

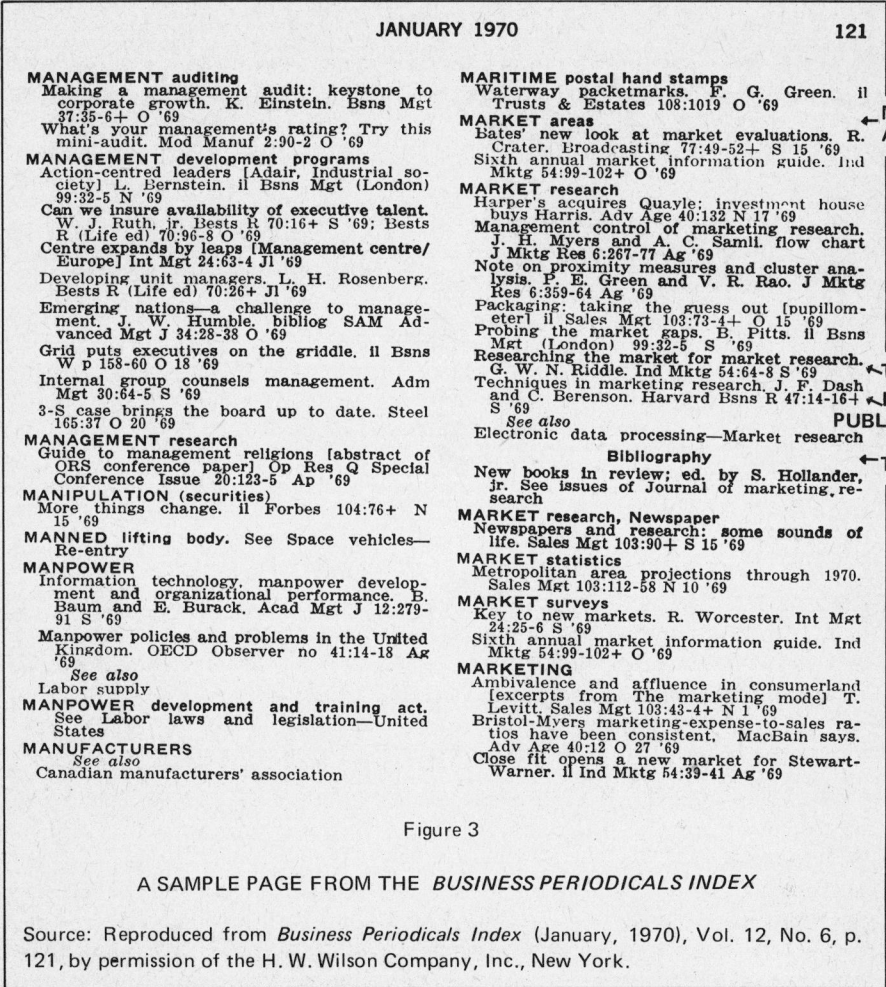

JANUARY 1970 **121**

MANAGEMENT auditing
Making a management audit: keystone to corporate growth. K. Einstein. Bsns Mgt 37:35-6+ O '69
What's your management's rating? Try this mini-audit. Mod Manuf 2:90-2 O '69

MANAGEMENT development programs
Action-centred leaders [Adair, Industrial society] L. Bernstein. il Bsns Mgt (London) 99:32-5 N '69
Can we insure availability of executive talent. W. J. Ruth, jr. Bests R 70:16+ S '69; Bests R (Life ed) 70:96-8 O '69
Centre expands by leaps [Management centre/Europe] Int Mgt 24:63-4 Jl '69
Developing unit managers. L. H. Rosenberg. Bests R (Life ed) 70:26+ Jl '69
Emerging nations—a challenge to management. J. W. Humble. bibliog SAM Advanced Mgt J 34:28-38 O '69
Grid puts executives on the griddle. il Bsns W p 158-60 O 18 '69
Internal group counsels management. Adm Mgt 30:64-5 S '69
3-S case brings the board up to date. Steel 165:37 O 20 '69

MANAGEMENT research
Guide to management religions [abstract of ORS conference paper] Op Res Q Special Conference Issue 20:123-5 Ap '69

MANIPULATION (securities)
More things change. il Forbes 104:76+ N 15 '69

MANNED lifting body. See Space vehicles—Re-entry

MANPOWER
Information technology, manpower development and organizational performance. B. Baum and E. Burack. Acad Mgt J 12:279-91 S '69
Manpower policies and problems in the United Kingdom. OECD Observer no 41:14-18 Ag '69
See also
Labor supply

MANPOWER development and training act. See Labor laws and legislation—United States

MANUFACTURERS
See also
Canadian manufacturers' association

MARITIME postal hand stamps
Waterway packetmarks. F. G. Green. il Trusts & Estates 108:1019 O '69 ◄—MAJOR

MARKET areas — AREA
Bates' new look at market evaluations. R. Crater. Broadcasting 77:49-52+ S 15 '69
Sixth annual market information guide. Ind Mktg 54:99-102+ O '69

MARKET research
Harper's acquires Quayle; investment house buys Harris. Adv Age 40:132 N 17 '69
Management control of marketing research. J. H. Myers and A. C. Samli. flow chart J Mktg Res 6:267-77 Ag '69
Note on proximity measures and cluster analysis. P. E. Green and V. R. Rao. J Mktg Res 6:359-64 Ag '69
Packaging: taking the guess out [pupillometer] il Sales Mgt 103:73-4+ O 15 '69
Probing the market gaps. B. Pitts. il Bsns Mgt (London) 99:32-5 S '69
Researching the market for market research. ◄—TITLE
G. W. N. Riddle. Ind Mktg 54:64-8 S '69
Techniques in marketing research. J. F. Dash ◄—FACTS OF
and C. Berenson. Harvard Bsns R 47:14-16+ PUBLICATION
S '69
See also
Electronic data processing—Market research

Bibliography ◄—TOPIC
New books in review; ed. by S. Hollander, jr. See issues of Journal of marketing, research

MARKET research, Newspaper
Newspapers and research: some sounds of life. Sales Mgt 103:90+ S 15 '69

MARKET statistics
Metropolitan area projections through 1970. Sales Mgt 103:112-58 N 10 '69

MARKET surveys
Key to new markets. R. Worcester. Int Mgt 24:25-6 S '69
Sixth annual market information guide. Ind Mktg 54:99-102+ O '69

MARKETING
Ambivalence and affluence in consumerland [excerpts from The marketing mode] T. Levitt. Sales Mgt 103:43-4+ N 1 '69
Bristol-Myers marketing-expense-to-sales ratios have been consistent, MacBain says. Adv Age 40:12 O 27 '69
Close fit opens a new market for Stewart-Warner. il Ind Mktg 54:39-41 Ag '69

Figure 3

A SAMPLE PAGE FROM THE *BUSINESS PERIODICALS INDEX*

Source: Reproduced from *Business Periodicals Index* (January, 1970), Vol. 12, No. 6, p. 121, by permission of the H. W. Wilson Company, Inc., New York.

Listings include article title, author's name, journal title, volume number, page numbers, and publication date. All this information is illustrated in Figure 3. A brief explanation of a typical entry will demonstrate how the index citation should be read. For example:

> Accountants, Law
> Accounting legislation of the future, J. L. Carey.
> J Account 123:46-51 Ja '67.

Translated into conventional English this entry tells you:

> An article on the legal aspects of accounting, entitled "Accounting Legislation of the Future" and written by J. L. Carey, has been published in Volume 123 of the *Journal of Accounting*, on pages 46-51 of the January 1967 issue.

Researchers agree that for the great majority of business subjects the *Business Periodicals Index* is the best single source of information and the logical starting point for all business, economic, financial, accounting, and related study. It indexes periodicals in the fields of

accounting
advertising and public relations
automation
banking
communications
economics
finance and investments
insurance
labor
management
marketing
taxation
specific businesses, industries, and trades

The *Business Periodicals Index* does not cover pamphlets and government reports to any significant extent. Fortunately for the researcher, the *Public Affairs Information Service Bulletin* indexes publications from more than 900 sources. It is published weekly from September through July and fortnightly in August; one issue is omitted in December. The issues are cumulatively indexed five times a year, and the final annual cumulative index is bound. The *Bulletin* offers a selected list of the latest books, pamphlets, government publications, reports of public and private agencies, and periodical articles relating to economic and social conditions, public administration, and international relations, according to subject.

It is a particularly good source for study in areas of business that involve government action, for example, minimum-wage laws, antitrust activities, and labor negotiations.

There is also the *Monthly Catalogue of United States Government Publications,* published monthly and cumulatively indexed annually. It provides comprehensive coverage of reports by various government agencies, many of which publish a great deal of material of primary and secondary interest to researchers in business areas. The entries include U. S. Government Printing Office catalogue number, price (if any), title, issuing agency, and whether or not it is available at Federal depository libraries. There are many such depositories across the nation, often housed in university libraries (see discussion later in this chapter).

The annual *Engineering Index* provides references to technically oriented publications in engineering, chemistry, and physics; many of them are not included in any of the indexes already described but do offer important, though limited, coverage of the commercial aspects of technological industries and problems. Relevant government publications and those of research laboratories and experimental stations in these fields are also indexed. In addition to listing data in the form common to the other indexes, the *Engineering Index* provides a brief summary of each article.

The *Applied Science and Technology Index* is similar in frequency of publication, format, type of information, and so on to the *Business Periodicals Index*. It is useful for its coverage of trade and technical publications that other indexes do not include. For example, the *Business Periodicals Index* lists articles from the leading *general* business magazines of the chemical industry, whereas the *Applied Science and Technology Index* also lists journals dealing with the business problems of specific segments of that industry, for example, solvents, adhesives, paints, and the like.

The *Readers' Guide to Periodical Literature* is a valuable reference for general periodicals. It is essential for supplementary material in many business studies. It is published twice a month, except in July and August, when it appears monthly, and it is cumulatively indexed quarterly and annually.

The *Insurance Index* is a monthly and annual index of articles on insurance, with cross references to such related business areas as accounting, management, advertising, and office management.

The Commerce Clearing House, Inc., publishes a cumulatively indexed, loose-leaf bulletin entitled *Accounting Articles;* it describes articles, notes, and comments appearing in current accounting and business periodicals. It is indexed by major subject division and by author. The major subject divisions are

accounting principles and practices
statements and reports
cost accounting
budgeting
auditing
management services
public accounting practice
accounting education

A representative page is shown in Figure 4.

The Commerce Clearing House also publishes separate indexes for

Federal taxes
state taxes
foreign taxes
banking
insurance
social security

labor

securities

business, including atomic energy, bankruptcy, corporate law, government contracts, installment credit, pension plans, and trade regulation

carriers and utilities

legislation

8-65
Report 6   **Current Articles—Report 6**   **9121**

ments are centered around the ten generally accepted auditing standards which have been approved and adopted by the members of the AICPA.

¶ 9438   Audit Programs and Planning

Table of Descriptions

Data processing and computers 22	Uniform Commercial Code . . .	.92
Management relations 56	Year-end problems . . .	.97
New Zealand 605		

.22 DATA PROCESSING AND COMPUTERS.—See also ¶ 9473.25.

Back reference: ¶ 5100.22.

Added Demands on the Auditor. Thomas I-Yao Chen. 41 Auditgram, April, 1965, pp. 12-14, 46.—In the computer, the auditor has a powerful tool which he can use to improve his efficiency. However, the internal bank auditor must keep in mind the cost relative to the protection when determining the adequacy of internal controls over data processing. Proper planning, reliability of the program, separation of duties and the use of the computer as an auditing aid are discussed.

An Auditor Faces the Computer. E. Hampton Morgan. 41 Auditgram, June, 1965, pp. 8-12.—A number of various aspects of automation auditing are covered in this article. These include problems of volume, reviewing programs, auditing through or around the computer, record protection, operational audits, audit responsibilities, and the auditing objectives. It is concluded that in auditing a computer operation the auditor is auditing an operational function of the bank or auditing a function which has been placed on the computer. In doing so the auditor is using the computer as a tool to perform a better and more complete audit.

Figure 4

A SAMPLE PAGE FROM *ACCOUNTING ARTICLES*

Source: Reproduced from *Accounting Articles,* Report 6 (August, 1965), p. 1921, by permission of the Commerce Clearing House, Inc., Chicago.

The *Accountants' Index* has been published annually since 1920, and a supplement is published every two years. Its format is similar to those of the *Business Periodicals Index* and others described here. It lists published materials of interest to the accounting profession, including books, articles, and government publications, by author's name, subject, and title. Information on the publisher, place of publication, date, and number of pages is also given. Addresses of publishers and periodicals are contained in a directory at the end of the volume.

The *American Economic Association Index,* published irregularly, covers eighty-nine English-language economics journals. It also includes journals on subjects of economic importance, like agriculture, population, health, welfare, and regional planning. In addition, researchers will find references to comments, replies, papers delivered before professional associations, reports of symposia, notes, and subject bibliographies. The twenty-three main categories of the *American Economic Association Index* are

> scope and method of economics
> economic theory, including monetary theory
> economic systems
> history of economic thought
> economic history
> general contemporary economic conditions, policy, and planning
> mathematical, statistical, and other analytic tools
> social accounting and statistical data
> money, credit, and banking
> public finance
> international economics
> economic fluctuations and stabilization policy
> war and defense economics
> business organization and managerial economics
> industrial organization and public policy
> agriculture
> natural resources and land economics
> population
> labor economics
> consumer economics
> health, education, and welfare
> regional planning and development and housing
> unclassified

The New York Times Index lists only articles published in *The New York Times.* It is published twice a month and is cumulatively indexed annually. The data are classified alphabetically and within each entry chronologically. Its utility for business researchers rests on *The Times'* extremely wide coverage of economic, financial, and business news. The articles themselves are readily available on microfilm in libraries throughout the nation.

The Wall Street Journal is the nation's largest daily business and financial newspaper. Because its coverage is so comprehensive *The Wall Street Journal Index,* published annually, is very useful.

Other Important Sources. In addition to books and articles, business researchers can make profitable use of several other library resources.

There are thousands of *directories,* covering such broad ranges of subject matter that, in many business studies, several can be very useful, for example, in compiling lists of companies and executives for a questionnaire. Some directories are specialized according to industry, for example, *Chemical Week Buyers Guide;* some according to function, for example, *Poor's Register of Directors and Executives;* and some according to company size, for example, *Dun & Bradstreet Million Dollar Directory.* There are even directories of directories.

The kind of information furnished by a well-known business directory can be illustrated by a buying guide, *MacRae's Blue Book,* published annually in Chicago. It contains an alphabetical list of manufacturers and their products. In addition, the total assets of each firm are noted. More important, there is also an alphabetical list of raw materials giving names, addresses, and other relevant information about the manufacturers who use them. Another section lists trade names and the firms that own them. This book enables the purchasing director to select vendors of various kinds from a limited geographic area, in order to reduce transportation costs. It also helps in preparing a list of acceptable bidders.

The four volumes of *American Manufacturers* include 10,000 pages of purchasing information. They list most products made by almost all manufacturers in the United States, as well as carrying product-descriptive advertising by 12,000 companies.

Poor's Register of Directors and Executives lists key corporate officials in utilities, industrial, mining, railroads, banks and insurance companies, and financial and investment institutions, as well as top personnel of major law firms. It is published annually, but supplements are issued in May, August, and November.

The tremendous volume of business literature has engendered several popular devices for reducing it to manageability. The *annotated bibliography* is one. It is a published list of articles, books, or both that an organization (frequently a trade or professional association) or specialist (scholar or consultant) has culled from the mass of available references. Aside from standard bibliographical data, many bibliographies also outline the approaches and distinctive features or contributions of the works listed. The American Management Association and other business groups have published a number of valuable bibliographies in recent years.

Most large corporations in the United States are publicly owned. Their stocks are generally traded in regulated markets, and they are obliged to file comprehensive *annual reports* and quarterly reports as well. The table of contents of a typical report lists a business summary of the firm's business for the period, the officers and directors, a report from the president, details of operations by division, consolidated financial statements (including a balance sheet, income account, and a five- or ten-year financial summary), and assessments by the auditor.

Business *dictionaries* offer concise information on relevant subjects. Among the most widely used are

Frank Henius, *The Dictionary of Foreign Trade* (Englewood Cliffs, New Jersey: Prentice-Hall, Inc., 1947)

Eric L. Kohler, *A Dictionary for Accountants* (Englewood Cliffs, New Jersey: Prentice-Hall, Inc., 1963)

Harold Lazarus, *American Business Dictionary* (New York: Philosophical Library, Inc., 1957)

Glenn Munn, *Encyclopedia of Banking and Finance* (Boston: Bankers Publishing Company, 1962)

H. S. Sloan and A. J. Zurcher, *A Dictionary of Economics* (New York: Barnes & Noble, Inc., 1953)

Encyclopedic Dictionary of Business (Englewood Cliffs, New Jersey: Prentice-Hall, Inc., 1953)

Encyclopedic Dictionary of Real Estate (Englewood Cliffs, New Jersey: Prentice-Hall, Inc., 1955)

Thomson's Dictionary of Banking (New York: Philosophical Press, 1952)

Business and financial services supply current information of interest to business organizations. Most important, they forecast trends in commodity prices, production, income, industry sales, and so on. Their offerings include extensive presentation of quantitative data, which are invaluable in business research.

Moody's Investors' Service, Inc., provides corporate and financial news and statistical and analytical sources in many fields. Its *Stock Survey, Advisory Reports, Investors' Advisory Service, Dividend Record, Bond Record,* and *Handbook of Common Stocks* are very valuable. Other annual investment publications issued by Moody's Investors' Service cover industrials, public utilities, railroads, government and municipal bonds, and banks (insurance, real estate, and investment trusts). Each contains detailed data on companies or governments that issue securities. Corporate information includes history, organization, operations, and financial statements. Supplements provide current material.

Standard and Poor's Corporation offers individual industry surveys (with financial and industrial analyses), *Outlook* (securities), *Bond Outlook, Called Bond Record,* stock reports (including over-the-counter sales and regional exchanges) and *Listed Bond Reports Corporation Manual* is issued monthly and indexed cumulatively.

United Business Service publishes business, financial, and commodity analyses and forecasts. Specific purchasing advice is given every week on the "Commodity Forecast" page. The biweekly "Buyer's Guide" gives clear and definite price forecasts on more than 100 important basic materials. A complete summary of important commodity-price trends—with charts and statistics—is presented quarterly, as are retail-price forecasts for consumers. The quarterly "Table of Commodity Price Changes" is another major feature that helps the purchasing agent keep his buying and inventory policies abreast of changing conditions.

The Research Institute of America publishes *Research Institute Report,* which discusses current economic and legislative developments affecting business.

Dun & Bradstreet, Inc., compiles credit information and reports, information on collections, general business information, and foreign-trade reports; a subsidiary publishes *Dun's Review* (a monthly business magazine), and several other journals.

Commerce Clearing House, Inc., offers tax, labor, business, financial, and legal reports in loose-leaf form. Prentice-Hall Looseleaf Services publishes materials on taxation, labor, government regulation of business, government contracts, miscellaneous financial services, and so on.

Many *handbooks* have been published on specific areas of business. Some of the most widely used are

George W. Aljian, *Purchasing Handbook* (New York: McGraw-Hill Book Co., Inc., 1959)

Credit Research Foundation, *Credit Management Handbook* (Homewood, Illinois: Richard D. Irwin, Inc., 1958)

Albert Wesley Frey, *Marketing Handbook* (New York: Ronald Press Co., 1965)

Carl Heyel, *Encyclopedia of Management* (New York: Reinhold Publishing Corporation, 1963)

Wyman P. Fiske and John A. Beckett, *Industrial Accountant's Handbook* (Englewood Cliffs, New Jersey: Prentice-Hall, Inc., 1955)

J. K. Lasser, *Handbook of Accounting Methods* (Princeton, New Jersey: D. Van Nostrand Co., 1964)

Jules I. Bogen, *Financial Handbook* (New York: (Ronald Press Co., 1964)

Harold B. Maynard, *Industrial Engineering Handbook* (New York: McGraw-Hill Book Co., Inc., 1963)

Florence Peterson (ed.), *Handbook of Labor Unions* (Washington, D.C.: American Council of Public Affairs, 1944)

George B. Carson (ed.), *Production Handbook* (New York: Ronald Press Co., 1958).

Finally, there are *United States government publications,* among which many of the most useful are published by the U. S. Department of Commerce Bureau of the Census.[2] The Bureau will also tabulate data for special purposes at cost. The *Census of Population* has been prepared every ten years since 1790. Population growth, population characteristics, birth and death rates, and migration are covered. The *Census of Manufactures* has been published every five years since 1948; it was first issued in 1810. Some of the many subjects on which data are included are sales and value added by industry, plant location, and percentage of industry output by product category. *The U.S. Industrial Outlook* brings this Census data up-to-date annually. The *Annual Survey of Manufactures* presents quarterly data for many industries. The *Census of Housing* has been issued every ten years since 1940. It covers structural characteristics, building conditions, occupancy, facilities, and financial data broken down by states, counties, metropolitan areas, and rural areas. New

---

[2]Refer to Erwin Esser Nemmers and John A. Myers, *Business Research* (New York: McGraw-Hill Book Co., Inc., 1966), Chapter 1.

housing starts have recently been added. The _Census of Business_ has been issued irregularly since 1929, but, starting in 1963, it is to appear every five years; it covers number of establishments, employment, and payroll data for retail, wholesale, and service trades. The _Census of Agriculture_ has been issued every five years since 1954 and goes back to 1840. It lists farms by type, acreage, facilities, land use, value of products, employment, expenditures, and so on. _Agricultural Statistics_ and the _Commodity Yearbook_ are published annually as supplement to the _Census of Agriculture._ The _Census of Minerals Industries_ was put on a five-year publishing schedule in 1963, but it was first published in 1850. It is supplemented by the _Minerals Yearbook_ (published by the U. S. Department of the Interior Bureau of Mines). The _Census_ includes minerals data by industrial classification, whereas the _Yearbook_ classifies data by product. The _Census of Transportation_ was published for the first time in 1963. It includes data on commodities by class of transportation, passenger transportation, truck and bus information. _Historical Statistics of the United States from Colonial Times to 1957_ includes data in 3,000 series going as far back as possible.

Among _other government publications_ is _Business Cycle Developments,_ a monthly report on seventy economic indicators and supplementary data, issued by the Department of Commerce. The _Economic Report of the President_ to Congress has been printed annually since 1947. It contains many tables to supplement the text, which is prepared by the President's Council of Economic Advisers. The _Federal Reserve Bulletin_ is published monthly by the Federal Reserve Board. Financial data on domestic and foreign banking are presented, along with key economic indexes. _Statistics of Income,_ based on income-tax returns, is published annually by the U. S. Treasury Department Internal Revenue Service.

Libraries

Once you know what information you need and the journal, book, or the like in which it appears, you are still faced with the problem of where to find the journals, directories, books, indexes, and so on. There are five main places to look.

Municipal and Other Public Libraries. The public library is, of course, an obvious place to look. Public-library systems in most large cities include lending and research libraries that are usually quite good. In fact, the Cleveland Public Library and the Newark, New Jersey, Free Public Library's business branch both publish business bibliographies.

Some of the most important "public" libraries for business are operated by the U. S. Department of Commerce. There are forty-two of them located in major cities across the nation; their collections are largely limited to United States government publications.

Government Libraries. The Federal government also supports a network of libraries in its various bureaus and agencies in Washington, D.C., for example, the libraries of the Federal Reserve Board and Federal Trade Commission.

Although these collections are highly specific and limited to the fields of interest of the supporting agencies, they are extremely comprehensive in those fields. State libraries will often furnish by mail or telephone information that does not require extended research.

Libraries in Universities and Business Firms. The resources of his own university libraries are available to the student; through them he may also be able to arrange access to libraries at other universities or in business firms, either directly or through interlibrary loans. Many large firms maintain excellent collections of both business and technical material relevant to their industries. Other companies or libraries can often arrange to borrow required materials. Trade publications in particular frequently maintain outstanding libraries of materials of interest to their readers. This information is not just for the use of their editorial staffs, but is almost always made available to students who request it. Generally, their staffs will photostat tables, compile statistics, prepare economic forecasts, and go to a great deal of time and expense to answer a query from anyone with a legitimate interest. There is usually no charge for such assistance.

Institutional Libraries. In large cities special libraries are often maintained by institutions, some of which are open to the public. Many are affiliated with major universities. In New York City, for example, the libraries of the American Museum of Natural History and the New York Botanical Garden are affiliated with the Columbia University Library. Through interlibrary loans students of the universities thus may have access to special collections on medicine, engineering, biology, chemistry, physics, finance, economics, law, accounting, life insurance, and the like.

Libraries of Trade and Professional Associations. Trade and professional associations often maintain excellent collections relevant to their fields of interest. These groups are dedicated to assisting members as well as all those who have an interest in that particular field. Many, like the American Institute of Accountants and the National Association of Accountants, also publish current bibliographies. An outstanding reference on trade associations is *National Associations of the United States,* published by the U. S. Department of Commerce in 1949, which presents details on all trade associations, including key officials. *The Encyclopedia of American Associations* is a standard reference guide to 9,000 associations and professional societies.

Bibliography

Cowan, Edwin T., *Sources of Business Information* (rev. ed.; Los Angeles: University of California Press, 1964), pp. xii + 330.

Executives' Guide to Information Sources (Detroit: Business Guides Company, 1965), pp. 2467. A detailed listing for management personnel of 2,300 business and business-related subjects, with records of periodicals, organizations, bureaus, directories, bibliographies, and other sources for each.

Johnson, H. Webster, and Stuart W. McFarland, *How to Use the Business Library: With Sources of Business Information* (2nd ed.; Cincinnati: South-Western Publishing Co., 1957), pp. iv + 154.

Manley, Marian C., *Business Information: How to Find and Use It* (New York: Harper & Brothers, 1955), pp. xvi + 265.

Schmeckebier, L., and R. B. Eastin, *Government Publications and Their Use* (Washington, D.C.: Brookings Institution, 1961), pp. xi + 476.

chapter 4
research design and analysis

Research in business and economics has changed radically in the past decade. A major characteristic of this change is the use of statistical techniques and concepts in both the formulation of research designs and in the analysis of the data obtained.

A full treatment of the use of these quantitative methods is not possible in a book this size; the subject is far too complex. Indeed, most of the fine textbooks on the subject of research design and analysis that have been published in recent years are considerably longer than this book.

Instead, we shall indicate the nature of *some* of the research planning and design tools available and refer interested readers to the works cited at the end of this chapter for details of these and other methods.

Research Design

After he has selected his research topic, the investigator must devise an efficient approach to the collection of information relevant to his purpose. This efficient approach is generally termed a "research design," and there are many different types.

Exploratory Studies. Initial research aimed at narrowing the topic and developing a hypothesis can simultaneously provide ideas for a more structured and rigorous attack upon the problem. For this purpose a study of secondary sources of information is quite valuable. Exploratory studies often take an eclectic path through the literature, in an attempt to find critical parameters and to acquaint the investigator with the problem area.

Descriptive Studies. Some hypotheses or research purposes emphasize fact finding without resort to experimentation. They differ from exploratory studies in the rigor with which they are designed and carried out. Exploratory studies are deliberately flexible so that ideas and hypotheses can be generated, whereas descriptive studies are carefully designed to ensure that as many relevant facts as possible are collected with the least effort. For example, on the basis of exploratory studies, a manufacturer of wrist watches may find that teen-agers are concerned less about quality and accuracy than about design; a descriptive study, however, would aim to determine precisely which elements are attractive to teen-agers, whether this preference is national or regional, and so on.

Experimental Studies. Sophisticated research in business and economics involves "experimental designs." This term signifies those procedures aimed at measuring cause-and-effect relationships, rather than merely at describing situations. In very general terms, it signifies those techniques "in which one or more variables are manipulated under conditions which permit the collection of data which show the effects, if any, of such variables in unconfused fashion."[1] Consequently, a great deal of effort is devoted by researchers to setting up situations that permit them to measure and record accurately what happens when specified variables are deliberately changed.

Over the years a number of standard designs—as well as some that are highly specialized—have been developed for many situations in which experimentation is required. One of the simplest is called the "before-after design," which is illustrated below.

Assume that a packer of tuna fish wants to determine the effect upon sales of a change in the design of the label on the can of tuna. First, the researcher measures the present level of sales (denoted here as y_1); then the labels are changed and he again measures the sales (now denoted as y_2). Finally he analyzes the results to learn what has been the effect of the label change, that is, he subtracts y_2 from y_1, or vice versa.

Before-After Design

Tuna sales before any experimentation	$= y_1$
Is an experiment initiated (label change)?	Yes
Tuna sales after the experiment	$= y_2$
The effect of the experiment	$= y_2 - y_1$

In the simplest of all standard designs the "before" measurement (y_1) is not taken; only the "after" measurement (y_2) is recorded. In more complex designs, control groups—samples on which *no* experimentation is carried out—are used, and other procedures are also followed in attempts to avoid and minimize many pitfalls and shortcomings of experimental research. A concise presentation of these standard designs is presented in Table 1.[2]

There are, of course, many frequently employed research designs that are not shown in Table 1. For example, there is the well-known Latin-square design, which permits the experimenter to ". . . control simultaneously two dependent variables, such as store size, time period, or region, which might materially affect responses of test units; it thus permits removal of their effects

[1] Harper W. Boyd, Jr., and Ralph Westfall, *Marketing Research: Text and Cases* (rev. ed.; Homewood, Illinois: Richard D. Irwin, Inc., 1964), p. 93.

[2] Claire Selltiz, *et al., Research Methods in Social Relations* (rev. ed.; New York: Holt, Rinehart and Winston, 1959), p. 110.

Table 1   Types of Experimental Design

Condition	1 "After Only"		2 "Before-After" with Single Group	3 "Before-After" with Interchangeable Groups		4 "Before-After" with One Control Group	
	Experimental Group	Control Group	Experimental Group	Experimental Group	Control Group	Experimental Group	Control Group
Prior selection of groups	Yes	Yes	Yes	Yes	Yes	Yes	Yes
"Before" measurement	No	No	Yes (y_1)	No	Yes (y'_1)	Yes (y_1)	Yes (y'_1)
Exposure to experimental variables	Yes	No	Yes	Yes	Perhaps	Yes	No
Exposure to uncontrolled events	Yes	Yes	Yes	Yes	Yes	Yes	Yes
"After" measurement	Yes (y_2)	Yes (y'_2)	Yes (y_2)	Yes (y_2)	No	Yes (y_2)	Yes (y'_2)
Change	$d = y_2 - y'_2$		$d = y_2 - y_1$	$d = y_2 - y_1$		$d = y_2 - y_1$	$d' = y'_2 - y'_1$

Condition	5 "Before-After" with Two Control Groups			6 "Before-After" with Three Control Groups			
	Experimental Group	Control Group I	Control Group II	Experimental Group	Control Group I	Control Group II	Control Group III
Prior selection of groups	Yes	Yes	Yes	Yes	Yes	Yes	Yes
"Before" measurement	Yes (y_1)	Yes (y'_1)	No ($y''_1 = \frac{y_1 + y'_1}{2}$)	Yes (y_1)	Yes (y'_1)	No ($y''_1 = \frac{y_1 + y'_1}{2}$)	No ($y'''_1 = \frac{y_1 + y'_1}{2}$)
Exposure to experimental variables	Yes	No	Yes	Yes	No	Yes	No
Exposure to uncontrolled events	Yes	Yes	Yes	Yes	Yes	Yes	Yes
"After" measurement	Yes (y_2)	Yes (y'_2)	Yes (y''_2)	Yes (y_2)	Yes (y'_2)	Yes (y''_2)	Yes (y'''_2)
Change	$d = y_2 - y_1$	$d' = y'_2 - y'_1$	$d'' = y''_2 - y''_1$	$d = y_2 - y_1$	$d' = y'_2 - y'_1$	$d'' = y''_2 - y''_1$	$d''' = y'''_2 - y'''_1$
Interaction		$I = d - (d' + d'')$				$I = d - (d' + d'' - d''')$	

Source: reproduced with permission from: Claire Selltiz, et al., Research Methods in Social Relations (rev. ed.; New York: Holt, Rinehart and Winston, 1959), p. 110.

from the experimental error."[3] Latin-square designs usually involve relatively short time periods, and when an experiment is repeated soon after its initial completion, the effect of the activities of the first test period may carry over into the second. To avoid this problem, a variation of the Latin square, called the "double change-over design," has been developed.[4]

Other designs include balanced incomplete-block designs, randomized block designs, factorial designs, and so forth.

Sampling

Once a research design has been created, the investigator must apply it to a *sample* of the *universe* being studied, for in most cases a study of the relevant universe in its entirety is not feasible. Obviously, if a design calls for varying the price of tuna fish in sixty-four supermarkets, these markets must be selected from among all those in existence. The procedures for selecting samples are well known, but this section may introduce the prospective researcher to just a few important considerations in selecting a proper sample.

The objective in selecting a sample is usually to achieve fairly accurate representation of the population from which it is taken. If we are studying the effects of price changes upon the food consumption of retired schoolteachers, we must be sure that the sample includes only retired schoolteachers and no electricians, employed schoolteachers, or used-car salesmen.

Once the sample has been selected and the research design implemented, the characteristics of the *universe* must be estimated from those measured for the sample. The universe is the total category under consideration, that is, all drug stores in cities of less than 100,000 population. For example, if we find that a 10-percent rise in the price of tuna fish has caused our retired teachers to decrease their tuna consumption by 15 percent (arithmetic mean), we then want to know whether or not this reaction is typical of *all* retired teachers. If it is not, to what extent does it deviate from what the reactions of *all* retired schoolteachers would be if they were measured? How confident of our estimates can we be?

In analyzing our findings we also want to know such facts as the range of responses to the price rise (perhaps 0-72 percent decline in consumption) and the standard deviations, quartile deviations, and other measures of variation. *Measures of variation* tell us the extent to which statistical data are spread out or bunched.

The techniques for determining such measures of variation, as well as those for measures of location, are well known and are described in detail in textbooks on statistics, which also introduce such research tools as correlation analysis, regression analysis, and time-series analysis. In regression analysis two variables are related in such a way as to permit prediction of the value of one of

[3] Seymour Banks, *Experimentation in Marketing* (New York: McGraw-Hill Book Co., Inc., 1965), p. 115.

[4] *Ibid.*, pp. 135-148.

them from knowledge of the other.[5] We could thus use regression analysis to find the relationship between price and sales volume.

Time-series analysis is the statistical technique for studying fluctuations in data over specific time periods: usually a day, a month, or a year.[6] For example, the weekly population of New York City or the number of securities sold on the American Stock Exchange each week could be analyzed for the most recent ten-year period.

Conclusions

Preparing a report, thesis, or dissertation requires careful attention to research planning and analysis, as well as to the final job of putting words on paper in an interesting, grammatical, and useful form. In this chapter, we have briefly outlined *some* aspects of research design and statistical analysis of data; unfortunately, space does not permit us to be more than indicative. Those readers who require additional knowledge about these essential activities will find the textbooks listed in the bibliography very useful.

Bibliography

Banks, Seymour, *Experimentation in Marketing* (New York: McGraw-Hill Book Co., Inc., 1965), pp. xii + 275.

Brennan, Michael J., Jr., *Preface to Econometrics* (Cincinnati: South-Western Publishing Co., 1960), pp. x + 419.

Boyd, Harper W., Jr., and Ralph Westfall, *Marketing Research: Text and Cases* (rev. ed.; Homewood, Illinois: Richard D. Irwin, Inc., 1964), pp. xvii + 791.

Cochran, William G., *Sampling Techniques* (2nd ed.; New York: John Wiley & Sons, Inc., 1963), pp. xvii + 413.

Churchman, C. West, Russell L. Ackoff, and E. Leonard Arnoff, *Introduction to Operations Research* (New York: John Wiley & Sons, Inc., 1957), pp. x + 645.

Ferber, Robert, and P. J. Verdoorn, *Research Methods in Economics and Business* (New York: The Macmillan Co., 1962), pp. xiv + 573.

Frank, Ronald E., and Paul E. Green, *Quantitative Methods in Marketing* (Englewood Cliffs, New Jersey: Prentice-Hall, Inc., 1967), p. 118.

Fruchter, Benjamin, *Introduction to Factor Analysis* (Princeton, New Jersey: D. Van Nostrand Co., Inc., 1954), pp. xii + 280.

Goetz, Billy E., *Quantitative Methods: A Survey and Guide for Managers* (New York: McGraw-Hill Book Co., 1965), pp. xxix + 541.

Hansen, Kermit O., and George J. Brabb, *Managerial Statistics* (2nd ed.; Englewood Cliffs, New Jersey: Prentice-Hall, Inc., 1961), pp. viii + 342.

[5]Samuel B. Richmond, *Statistical Analysis* (2nd ed., New York: Ronald Press Co., 1964), pp. 424-474.

[6]*Ibid.*, pp. 346-398.

Kaplan, Lawrence J., *Elementary Statistics for Economics and Business* (New York: Pitman Publishing Corp., 1966), pp. xv + 297.

Kattsoff, Louis O., and Albert J. Simone, *Finite Mathematics* (New York: McGraw-Hill Book Co., Inc., 1965), pp. xiv + 407.

Kish, Leslie, *Survey Sampling* (New York: John Wiley & Sons, Inc., 1965), pp. xvi + 643.

Levin, Richard I., and C. A. Kirkpatrick, *Quantitative Approaches to Management* (New York: McGraw-Hill Book Co., Inc., 1965), pp. xiv + 365.

Mason, Robert D., *Statistical Techniques in Business and Economics* (Homewood, Illinois: Richard D. Irwin, Inc., 1967), pp. xii + 520.

Rummel, J. Francis, and Wesley C. Ballaine, *Research Methodology in Business* (New York: Harper & Row, 1963), pp. xvi + 359.

Selltiz, Claire, *et al.*, *Research Methods in Social Relations* (rev. ed.; New York: Holt, Rinehart and Winston, 1959), pp. xvi + 622.

Siegel, Sidney, *Nonparametric Statistics* (New York: McGraw-Hill Book Co., Inc., 1956), pp. xvii + 312.

Spurr, William A., and Charles P. Bonini, *Statistical Analysis for Business Decisions* (Homewood, Illinois: Richard D. Irwin, Inc., 1967), pp. xii + 743.

chapter 5
taking notes

Once you have become familiar with the pertinent library sources, you are ready to collect data from these sources. The success of your report, thesis, or dissertation depends directly upon the skill with which you cull significant data from the literature.

It is wise *not* to read your sources as you uncover them, for you probably will not yet have a very good idea of the relative value of all the sources that you may find. Instead, search the literature fairly completely first; then make a bibliography and arrange the sources in some logical order (chronologically, topically, or some other way; see Chapter 8). Then you will be in a far better position to draw material from the sources efficiently and with proper emphasis upon the truly important ones, rather than upon trivial ones.

Reading Your Sources

You read sources in a fashion quite different from that in which you read textbooks, novels, and the like. Ordinarily when you read you are not looking for *specific* facts and must therefore read nearly every word, in order to find items of significance. Research reading, however, involves looking for *specific* data that your preliminary outline and research have suggested are necessary. Even if you wanted to read all the material in every reference work, time limitations would not permit it. Thus, when you turn to a written source, you must make every effort to confine your reading to only those facts that you must have for your report.

Your search can be narrowed through careful use of the index, examination of the table of contents, scanning major and minor headings within chapters or parts of the work, skimming the material, reading chapter or article introductions and summaries, and so forth.

The question of how you can tell in advance what you are going to need arises, of course. Unless you have a good idea of that, the shortcuts described here cannot help much. The answer is to read as widely and generally as possible before selecting your topic, writing your prospectus, and constructing your outline. Such reading, combined with a broad knowledge of the field in which you are specializing, will provide the necessary perspective for efficient reading of sources. In addition, once you have constructed the rough outline, you should become thoroughly familiar with it, so that your specific information needs are firmly in mind at all times.

Useful Hints for Taking Good Notes

The experience of countless researchers can be summarized in seven valuable procedures.

Record Your Notes. Take notes on file cards 3 × 5 inches, 4 × 6 inches, or 5 × 8 inches or on half-sheets of 8½ × 11-inch typing paper (cut to 5½ × 8½ inches). Most researchers use cards for convenience and easy handling and filing. During your research and writing you will have to shuffle these cards hundreds of times; larger sizes are unwieldy and too bulky to carry around. Most students find the 4 × 6 or the 5 × 8-inch cards the best compromise between handling ease and maximum space.

Use an Outline Form. Be concise; abbreviate whenever possible (see Chapter 9 for a more complete discussion of outlines).

Use Ink, or Type. Penciled cards smudge from constant handling.

Use a Separate Card for Each Idea, Reference, or Whole Unit of Data. Each card should be keyed to a facet of your work or lowest-level heading in your outline. If the same reference offers information on two or more headings of your outline, put each on a different card. Key the note to the outline reference.

Use Only One Side of Card. If you use two sides, you will constantly have to turn cards over to find what is on the reverse sides. Most of your references will fit readily onto one or two card surfaces.

Do the Job Correctly from the Start. Enter the notes precisely and thoroughly while you have the source before you. Do not count on "filling in" at home. The chances are against you: memory lapses, lack of time, insufficient data, and the like will prevent you from producing first-rate note cards except while you have the material before you. Differentiate clearly between fact and opinion in order to avoid future confusion or error. Take enough notes initially so that you do not have to reexamine the source.

Be Consistent in Card Format. When the data are arranged in similar fashion on all cards, you will always know where to look for a certain fact like the author's name. In addition, inadvertent omissions of vital information will be immediately obvious.

What Note Cards Should Contain

All note cards *must* contain certain classes of information. These categories of data are listed below.

Label. The label should identify the *content* of the notes and their *relevance* to a particular part of your outline; the outline number and heading can be used in conjunction with other identifying words. If the relevant outline heading is "2.11–The Job Induction Program," and your notes are on follow-up interviews for such programs, then your label could be "2.11–Job Induction Program, Follow-Up Interviews."

The label should be at the very top of the card, in the upper left-hand corner. It is a good policy always to arrange the note cards according to these labels so that you can immediately determine which data are needed, which are superfluous, how important they may be, and whether or not one card's information agrees or disagrees with that of another.

For very lengthy and complex studies, there are cards that permit codes for labels and other descriptive and content data to be punched along the edges or on their face. Information retrieval is thus quick and accurate. The student should consult recent books on information retrieval that contain full discussions of these cards and their uses.

Call Numbers. Record library and call numbers so that you can easily recheck the source if necessary. As the various libraries in which you work may use different call-number systems, be sured to include the name of the library.

Footnote and Bibliographical References. It is essential to include full publication data on the source, as well as location of the noted material within the source, so that you may have all the data that you need to construct your bibliography and footnotes.

Remember the one significant difference between footnotes and bibliographical references: for the latter the page numbers of the *entire* source are recorded; for a footnote reference only the pages actually cited are noted. As your note cards must incorporate *both* number citations, use a system like the following to differentiate them: first, at the top of the note card, where the author's name, the source title, and so on are recorded, put the total number of pages; second, as you enter quotations, summaries, and so forth on the body of the card, preface them with the *specific* page numbers from which they are taken.

Body of the Note. Information taken from the source can be recorded as a summary, paraphrase, quotation, commentary, or any combination of them. Here are some examples and their explanations.

In a *summary* you substantially condense the relevant information in your own words. It is not difficult to do: there are very few ideas, views, collections of data, and the like that cannot be reduced to fewer words after careful analysis.

The difference between a summary and a *paraphrase* is that the latter does not emphasize condensation of the original work; instead, it is a simple rephrasing of the original material.

The author's exact words may be *quoted* for some reason (for comparison with another author's views, because they are too succinct or appropriate to be changed, and so on). Be sure, when you quote directly, that you place quotation marks around the relevant material; longer quotations may be indented instead. See Chapter 11 for more detailed discussion of quotations.

When you are *commenting* on the data in the source, rather than simply recording information, your note may take the form of a criticism, a question, a comparison, an evaluation, or the like.

A particular card does not have to be limited to any of these approaches. A *combination* may be necessary, but be sure to preserve the distinction among the various elements, so that you can credit the original source properly. It is good practice to summarize or comment as much as possible. Whenever you are writing your own comments on the same card as a summary, paraphrase, or quotation of the author's work, be especially careful to differentiate your work from his. You can use different-colored inks, underlining, both printing and writing or your own initials to indicate the beginning and end of each comment.

Evaluate Your Sources

Not every reference merits equal attention in reading and taking notes. To ensure the most reliable data for your research projects, it is sound practice to evaluate the reputation of the publisher, the reputation of the author, and the intention of the author. A *general* knowledge of your field will provide you with insight about the publishers, and good preliminary research will permit you to evaluate the accomplishments of an author, as well as his intention. An understanding of the latter is particularly important, for the same author can write both highly technical works for the specialist and general works for the layman.

When to Stop Taking Notes

You cannot go on reading and taking notes forever. Students often have great difficulty in determining when they have taken enough notes to begin the writing phase. A few guidelines may save you trouble.

1. Know your outline very well. When you do, you will be better able to *balance* the amounts of data that you accumulate; in general, avoid collecting ninety-seven note cards on one chapter and only twenty-seven on the next. If you have seventeen cards on "2.31—Compensation Planning in the Maturity Phase" and only three on "2.32—Inventory Policies in the Maturity Phase," you may be using poor judgment.

2. Stop collecting information when it merely repeats what you already have gathered from other sources.

3. Do not try to gather every single available fact on your subject. You are not going to write a twenty-volume work.

4. Be selective. As you cannot record and assimilate *all* relevant material, use only the best. When you are sure that you have enough

first-class material on some aspect of your subject, stop collecting more!

5. Remember that you can always go back for more data if you do not have enough and that most students gather several times as many data as they will need or use.

Keep Records of Your Search in the Sources

Keep a complete running record of the libraries, periodicals, and the like that you have consulted in your research. Otherwise you are likely at some time to go over the same ground again. If you stop a day's work after having searched the *Business Periodicals Index* from 1967 back through 1952, note it, so that you have a starting point for the next day.

Notes Unrelated to a Specific Source

Quite often a useful idea on organizing your cards, on a good person to consult, on a method for analyzing your results, and the like will occur to you. It is imperative that you record these ideas on note cards immediately so that you do not forget them. It is just these spontaneous ideas, arising from thorough immersion in your task, that often provide the most fruitful results.

chapter 6
interviewing

Interviews can be a source of information about *objective* events, conditions, practices, policies, and techniques. They are also immensely useful as a source of information on such *subjective* areas as attitudes, preferences, opinions, tastes, and emotional reactions.[1] Interviews also help to "open doors" to possible future employment.[2]

Interviews can usually be readily obtained, as authorities rarely refuse to see a student (especially a graduate student). But remember that the *results* of an interview depend in large part upon your own appearance, behavior, and preparation. The skill with which you ask questions will often influence the length of time allotted to you and the quality of the answers. Here are some tips on interviewing procedures.

First, *make a list* of people who must be interviewed, and eliminate those who would merely repeat information obtained from others. Try to learn some basic facts about each "interviewee" (title, education, business background).

It is one thing to say "make up a list of people who must be interviewed"; it is another, however, actually to go ahead and do it. A few hints may help. Begin, of course, by asking your instructor and other faculty members in your field for guidance. Also, examine the problem that you are trying to resolve very carefully. For example, if you are studying job induction in the chemical industry, then it is easy enough to make up a list of chemical industry firms which are located near you. Each of these organizations will probably have a personnel department; it is in this department that the individual whom you want to interview is generally located. A letter to the head of the personnel department, or a telephone inquiry, will usually get you the name of this individual.

Another approach is to examine the relevant literature and to list the names of authors who are accessible to you. You can also telephone or write to

---

[1] Many books and articles have been written on how to conduct successful interviews; an example is Walter V. Bingham and Bruce V. Moore, *How to Interview* (New York: Harper & Row, 1959).

[2] Leland Brown, *Effective Business Report Writing* (Englewood Cliffs, New Jersey: Prentice-Hall, Inc., 1955), p. 67.

the editors of suitable trade journals and to the secretaries of trade and professional associations related to your field of inquiry for suggestions on possible interviewees.

In addition to these sources, faculty members other than your instructor may be able to add names to your list. Finally, as described below, each interviewee should be asked to recommend others whose knowledge may shed light on your problem.

5128 East 75th Street
New York, N.Y. 10022

Full name
Position
Company
Location

Mr. John H. Jones
Vice President, Personnel
Enterprise Chemical Corporation
50 Wall Street
New York, N.Y. 10010

Dear Mr. Jones:

Personal identity

I am a candidate for the master's degree in marketing at Columbia University.

Thesis title

The title of my thesis is "Quantitative Techniques for Measuring Personnel Performance." I would appreciate an interview concerning subject matter essential for the completion of my research, that is, to discuss such techniques as used in your company.

Reason for interview

Permission for recording information

The results of the interview will not be recorded without your permission. I intend to collate the information with that obtained from others.

Distribution of results

I plan to distribute the conclusions reached on my thesis to those interviewed, upon request.

Time—alternative proposals

My classes are in the morning; I would therefore appreciate a conference any afternoon. If this is not possible, I can arrange to meet you at your convenience.

Sincerely,

Ralph L. Brown

Ralph L. Brown

Figure 5

A SAMPLE LETTER REQUESTING AN INTERVIEW

While you are compiling your interview list, note the names of people who can serve to *introduce you* to the potential respondents, to enhance your chances of obtaining worthwhile interviews.

Second, *write or telephone for an interview,* being sure to identify yourself and to state your objectives. Expedite arrangement of a mutually convenient time by offering a number of alternative choices. Figure 5 is an example of a good letter, requesting an interview.

In many instances it may seem preferable to telephone for an appointment; remember that the same information that you would have put into a letter must be given over the telephone. Whenever possible, show the respondent how the interview will benefit him too; keep in mind that the more clearly he sees "what's in it for him" the better are your chances of being granted the interview.

The interview itself can often be conducted over the telephone. This approach usually saves time and money. Of course, it has disadvantages too; for example, you cannot always reach the desired individual by telephone, some questions cannot be answered satisfactorily in the brief time span of a telephone conversation (records may have to be examined, for example); it is impossible to see the reaction of the respondent to the questions; depth interviews cannot be readily conducted; and so on.[3]

Third, *identify yourself.* Indicate your status at the university, the title of the study, and the need for a conference.

Fourth, *state your objectives.* Tell why it is necessary for you to have the interview and the reason for selecting him.

Fifth, *assure interviewees of your discretion.* Assure them that you will not quote them without permission or identify their firms specifically in any way. All information received during the interviews should be combined with other data in such a way that the composite results can be classified and analyzed without violating confidences granted to you. Offer to submit to each interviewee for his prior approval a copy of all quoted or paraphrased statements. If he does not grant his approval, you can still use the data as general background information.

Sixth, *offer to send the interviewees your conclusions.* The interviewees may find your conclusions of direct interest; ask them if they would like to see copies of the final chapter or section of your manuscript.

Seventh, *take notes at each interview.* Most respondents understand the student's needs and are not offended by note-taking. But do not plan to tape-record an interview unless previous permission has been given. When he is conscious of being recorded, the interviewee may guard so carefully against "slips of the tongue" or "personal opinions" that his answers become mechanical and relatively uninformative. A good way to take notes at an interview is on file cards. (To be sure that each card can be readily used when it is time to

---

[3] Mildred Parten, *Surveys, Polls and Samples* (New York: Harper & Brothers, 1950), pp. 91-93.

organize your notes for writing the manuscript, key it to your outline; see Chapter 9.)

Eighth, *ask only essential questions.* It is wise to prepare a series of questions to be answered in each interview. Do not ask a factual question that can be answered through research in published sources; obtain this kind of information *before* the interview. Sometimes it is wise to submit your questions in advance of the interview, particularly when preparation is needed for a good reply. Ask as few questions as possible. In the limited time of an interview it is better to cover a few important questions thoroughly. It is wise, however, to include questions that cross-check one another. The answers can then be used to gauge the consistency and sincerity of the person interviewed. Try out your questions before the interview. Ask fellow students or a faculty adviser if the questions seem to them essential, lucid, and pertinent. In fact, it is a good idea to rehearse the entire interview, in order to gauge times and sequence of the questions.

Ninth, *make every effort* during the interviews themselves *to gain the confidence of the interviewee.* Wide knowledge of the subject matter is tremendously helpful in generating discussion of mutual interest. You should not evaluate, praise, or criticize an interviewee's answers. A friendly and diplomatic attitude is important. At times, however, the interviewer might want to challenge the respondent or in some way differ with him in order to elicit a spontaneous and valuable response.

Tenth, *do not waste time on irrelevancies.* Never forget that, although your interview may start well, it can be "shut off" by boredom on the part of the interviewee or the sudden call of business matters for his attention. If you digress from the main topic, you may never have time to come back to it. Before you conclude your interview, run over your checklist of questions, to be sure that none has been omitted.

Eleventh, *thank the interviewee,* and let him know that he has contributed materially to your research. Many researchers also send brief follow-up notes thanking those who have helped them.

Twelfth, *stop interviewing when you begin to receive the same answers.* There is a practical limit to the number of people whom you can interview. When the answers are no longer adding significantly to what you already have, then it is time to stop interviewing. Some repetition cannot, of course, be avoided, but excess interviewing should be minimized.

Bibliography

Bassett, Glen A., *Practical Interviewing* (New York: American Management Association, 1965), p. 160.

Bingham, Walter V., and Bruce V. Moore, *How to Interview* (New York: Harper & Row, 1959), p. 277.

Boyd, Harper W., Jr. and Ralph Westfall, *Marketing Research: Text and Cases* (rev. ed.; Homewood, Illinois: Richard D. Irwin, Inc., 1964), pp. xvii + 791.

Brown, Leland, *Effective Business Report Writing* (2nd ed.; Englewood Cliffs, New Jersey: Prentice-Hall, Inc., 1955), pp. xvi + 446.

Kahn, Robert L., and Charles Cannell, *The Dynamics of Interviewing: Theory, Technique and Cases* (New York: John Wiley & Sons, Inc., 1957), p. 368.

Luck, David, Hugh Wales, and Donald Taylor, *Marketing Research* (Englewood Cliffs, New Jersey: Prentice-Hall, Inc., 1961), pp. x + 541.

Newman, Joseph W., *Motivation Research and Marketing Management* (Norwood, Massachusetts: Plimpton Press, 1957), pp. xii + 525.

Parten, Mildred, *Surveys, Polls and Samples* (New York: Harper & Brothers, 1950), pp. xii + 624.

Pittenger, Robert E., Charles Hockett, and John Danehy, *The First Five Minutes: A Sample of Microscopic Interview Analysis* (Ithaca, New York: P. Martineau, 1960), pp. ix + 264.

Richardson, Steven A., Barbara Dohrenwend, and David Klein, *Interviewing* (New York: Basic Books, Inc., 1965), pp. viii + 380.

Winfrey, Robley, *Technical and Business Report Preparation* (3rd ed.; Ames, Iowa: Iowa State University Press, 1962), pp. x + 340.

chapter 7
preparing and distributing a questionnaire

Questionnaires can be effective devices for securing information.[1,2] A questionnaire is a set of questions sent to a number of respondents especially to obtain statistically useful information. The questions are presented in an orderly arrangement, and space is provided for answers. You should use a questionnaire only after you are familiar enough with your topic to know the right questions to ask, how to phrase them, whom to send them to, and the like. Clearly, a great deal of study precedes the construction of a questionnaire.

Advantages of the Questionnaire

The questionnaire offers many advantages to business researchers. Information may be obtained from wide geographical areas at low cost. It is possible to canvass many authorities or organizations in a relatively short time and inexpensively, in direct contrast to the more cumbersome technique of personal interviewing. As questionnaires may be filled out at leisure, respondents may give more thought to them than is possible in a brief personal interview. Key business people who are personally inaccessible will often find the time to answer mail questionnaires, especially if they are assured that their names will not be used and that the information provided will be treated in such a way that no confidential company matters will be revealed. Questionnaires are extremely versatile and can be designed to shed light upon many business problems. Finally, questionnaire replies, in contrast to those in personal interviews, are not subject to any bias generated by personal interaction between interviewer and respondent—interviewer's appearance, tone, language, and conduct, for example.

Disadvantages of the Questionnaire

A major shortcoming of the questionnaire is that the rate of return may be quite low. This rate typically ranges from only 5 percent of the questionnaires distributed (for example, when the sample is not good or when the subject

[1] Mildred Parten, *Surveys, Polls and Samples* (New York: Harper & Brothers, 1950).

[2] Robert Ferber, Donald Blankertz and Sidney Hollander, Jr., *Marketing Research* (New York: Ronald Press Co., 1964).

under investigation is not particularly important to the respondent) to 55 percent (as when questionnaires are distributed to a very specific group with a special interest in the problem under investigation). Nor can you ever be sure who actually fills out the questionnaire; the addressee may turn it over to an assistant, a clerk, or a relative. It is difficult to phrase the questions so that they mean the same things to all respondents; some may interpret questions in unintended ways, which biases the response data. Because of the necessary brevity of most questionnaires, the answers tend to lack depth; for the same reason the area that can be covered in a questionnaire is circumscribed. The quality of the answers may suffer because full explanations are impossible.

Preparation of the Questionnaire

Your questionnaire will be mailed to individuals and organizations who are not paid for time and effort spent in completing it and who also receive questionnaires from governmental agencies, quasi-public agencies, publications, trade associations, charitable groups, other students, and research bureaus. Consequently, to assure the receipt of a relatively high percentage of returns, the characteristics described below should be embodied. Keep in mind that, even when you construct a superior questionnaire and send it to a representative sample of your population, your returns will seldom be more than 50 percent of the sample. A sample questionnaire is presented at the end of this chapter on pp. 52-54.

There are a number of guidelines for preparing a good questionnaire. First, it should be as brief as possible, never more than three typed pages. Long or involved questions elicit few replies. No question should be inserted that will not be used profitably in your written work.

Second, questions should be tested to ensure clarity of expression and thus avoid misinterpretation. Long and complicated questions should be avoided. Try to read the questions as if *you* were the recipient of the questionnaire. Try to avoid duplicating components of questions.

Third, the questions should be arranged in a coherent and logical sequence. Certain questions can often influence answers to subsequent questions.

Fourth, objective questions generate more responses than do essay questions. Recipients hesitate to prepare elaborate answers for a questionnaire, but many of them will readily check a "yes," a "no," or one choice from several alternatives. Allow enough space for longer answers if you must have them.

Fifth, as questionnaire results are generally tabulated, the questionnaire should be designed to facilitate such tabulation. For example, by numbering each question and each part of every question.

Sixth, put the questions of most interest to you first whenever possible within the framework of a logical sequence.

Seventh, put last the questions that are most difficult or embarrassing for the respondent. If he refuses to answer them at least you will have his answers to the earlier questions. But do not waste time asking for information that respondents cannot reasonably be expected to recall; or their personal motivations for certain activities, or other annoying questions.

Eighth, as the covering letter (see next section) may become separated from the questionnaire, be sure to place at the top of the first page of the questionnaire the following material: your name and address; the purpose of the study; the date by which you must have the reply; special instructions (if any) for completing the questionnaire; a guarantee of anonymity to the respondent if he wants it; and a statement of thanks for his cooperation.

Ninth, each questionnaire should have a "classification section" after the last formal question. There you ask the respondent to provide personal information that will permit you to assemble, tabulate, classify, and cross-classify responses from *all* the questionnaires. "Classification data" include age, sex, occupation, education, income, address, company name, company's business and products, annual sales, number of employees, and the like.

Tenth, review the final copy of the questionnaire carefully to eliminate mechanical errors, sloppiness, misspelled words, improper spacing, incorrect punctuation, and other errors.

Eleventh, the physical appearance of the questionnaire (and covering letter) are very important. Use fine bond paper, 8½ X 11 inches, and take pains to achieve an attractive layout. Use a photocopying or offset-printing process for reproduction; do *not* mimeograph your materials.

Finally, designing questionnaires is still more of an art than a science. Even experienced professional questionnaire writers must pretest and revise their work several times before it is ready for release. Pretesting involves mailing copies to a small representative sample from the same universe (the totality of potential respondents) from which the final sample will be drawn. The test may indicate ambiguous or unnecessary questions, and the like. These must be deleted or changed.

External Factors

Several factors greatly influence the extent and types of responses to a mail questionnaire, aside from the content of the questions themselves. You can maximize the quantity and quality of replies that you receive by remembering the following principles.

First, with each questionnaire enclose a self-addressed, stamped envelope for easy reply. The recipient will hesitate simply to throw away this expenditure by the student.

Second, send a covering letter on a separate sheet, explaining to the respondent why he has been selected: because of his position, his knowledge of the subject, his background, or his interest in the problem; as a result of random sampling of his socioeconomic group; or whatever the reason. Identify yourself as a candidate for a master's or doctoral degree or as a student. Tell the respondent the title and objectives of your study and why you need his

4422 Benson Avenue
Forest Hills, N.Y. 11375

February 14, 1970

Mr. Charles Barbett
Vice President, Personnel
Sampson Chemical Company
33 West 42 Street
New York, N.Y. 10036

Dear Mr. Barbett:

To achieve a better profit position, many chemical process industries firms have recently inaugurated substantial management-training programs. At the present, the results of several of these programs indicate that difficulty in properly setting training goals is one of the primary causes of management training inefficiency in the CPI.

The attached questionnaire is specifically designed to permit me to analyze this problem and can be readily completed by an executive of your personnel department. The information gathered in the study will be used only for comparative purposes; your company will not be identified with the results in any way if you so request.

The results of my studies for my master's thesis at the Columbia University School of Business will probably be published under the title, "The Techniques for Setting Management-Training Goals in the Chemical Process Industries." With your cooperation, my thesis will help to shed light on the problem of goal setting and provide valuable information for the chemical industry.

I would greatly appreciate your returning the filled-out questionnaire to me by March 15, 1970. For your convenience, a stamped and addressed envelope is enclosed.

I shall be glad to send you a copy of the summary, conclusions, and recommendations from my thesis if you will note your request on the questionnaire. Thank you for your assistance.

Sincerely yours,

Albert James Walker
Albert James Walker

Enclosure

Figure 6

A SAMPLE LETTER REQUESTING COMPLETION OF A QUESTIONNAIRE

cooperation. Be as informal as possible, and avoid stilted expressions. Also try, whenever possible, to show the respondent how he too will profit, directly or indirectly, from your research. Perhaps you will be shedding light on some problem affecting his industry, for example. Offer to send a summary of your findings upon request. Few respondents will bother to take advantage of your offer, but more will be inclined to fill out and return the questionnaire if you make it. Be sure to guarantee that the recipient's name and confidential replies will be revealed only with his permission.

Third, time the distribution of the questionnaire carefully. Few retailing people answer questionnaires in December, and accountants are very unresponsive in April. Be sure to mention the date by which you must have back the completed forms.

Fourth, mail the questionnaire to the "right" respondents. Your sample must be carefully prepared, and you must have the correct names and addresses of the individuals in it. The validity of the results will depend upon the representativeness of the sample and the techniques that you use in studying the data from that sample.

Fifth, if the percentage of returns is below a reasonable goal, a follow-up letter is in order. If questionnaires have been mailed to a small sample of the population and responses are extremely low, it is desirable to reexamine the questionnaire.

A Survey of Techniques Used for Setting Management-Training Goals in the Chemical-Process Industries

This questionnaire is being used to gather information for a study being conducted as a basis for preparing an M.B.A. thesis examining and evaluating the different methods currently used in setting management-training goals in the chemical-process industries. These data will be connected to the name of a company only with the permission of the respondent. In order to obtain the necessary information for this project, the cooperation of sales executives in the chemical field is needed.

Please fill in this questionnaire and send it, by March 15, 1970 to:

Albert James Walker
4422 Benson Avenue
Forest Hills, N.Y. 11375

Figure 7

A SAMPLE QUESTIONNAIRE

Figure 7 (Cont'd.)

NAME OF COMPANY _____

ADDRESS _____

No.   Street   City   State

NAME AND TITLE OF EXECUTIVE ANSWERING _____

(Leave blank if desired)

_____

Name

_____

Title

The name of this firm may (may not) be used with the data below.

1. What are the principal products sold by your company?_____

2. Are your sales   local _____   national _____

regional _____   other (specify) _____

3. What were the approximate total sales for your products last year?

      Under $500,000   _____

      $500,000-$999,999   _____

      $1,000,000-$4,999,999   _____

      $5,000,000-$24,999,999   _____

      $25,000,000-$100,000,000   _____

      Over $100,000,000   _____

4. Approximately how many people are considered to be management-level personnel? _____

5. Does your company establish management-training goals?

yes _____   no _____

6. If no, why?_____

_____

7. If yes, what method(s) do you use to set these goals?

name of method(s) _____

describe _____

_____

(If additional space is needed, please use the back of the last page of the questionnaire)

8. Who performs the job of training?

      a. personnel department _____

      b. experts from other company departments _____

      c. specialists from outside the firm _____

      d. other _____

Figure 7 (Cont'd.)

9. When is the training done?
    a. on company time _____
    b. on individual's time _____
    c. both _____

10. What percentage of your managerial personnel receives training each year?

    _____

11. I would appreciate any comments that you might care to make on areas to
    which this study can be extended, your opinions of the use of goals for
    training managers, and what you believe to be the key problems in setting
    these goals.

    I would also appreciate a copy of your company's organization chart.

    Thank you for your cooperation.

Questions in a Letter

Under certain circumstances, it is unnecessary to prepare an elaborate
questionnaire to secure essential information. A student can prepare a few
judiciously worded questions and request answers all in a one-page letter, but the
fundamental rules for successful responses to questionnaires also apply to such
letters.

Bibliography

Alevizos, John, P., *Marketing Research: Applications, Procedures and Cases*
(Englewood Cliffs, New Jersey: Prentice-Hall, Inc., 1959), pp. xi + 676.

Boyd, Harper W., Jr., and Ralph Westfall, *Marketing Research: Text and Cases*
(rev. ed.; Homewood, Illinois: Richard D. Irwin, Inc., 1964), pp.
xvii + 791.

Ferber, Robert, Donald F. Blankertz, and Sidney Hollander, Jr., *Marketing
Research* (New York: Ronald Press Co., 1964), pp. xi + 679.

Green, Paul E., and Donald S. Tull, *Research for Marketing Decisions* (Englewood Cliffs, New Jersey: Prentice-Hall, Inc., 1966), pp. viii + 532.

Holmes, Parker M., *Marketing Research* (Cincinnati: South-Western Publishing
Co., 1960), pp. x + 646.

Luck, David, Hugh Wales, and Donald Taylor, *Marketing Research* (Englewood
Cliffs, New Jersey: Prentice-Hall, Inc., 1961), pp. x + 541.

Madge, John, *The Tools of Social Science* (Garden City, New York: Doubleday
& Co., Inc., 1965), pp. xxxv + 362.

Parten, Mildred, *Surveys, Polls and Samples* (New York: Harper & Brothers,
1950), pp. xii + 624.

Schreier, Fred, *Modern Marketing Research: A Behavioral Science Approach* (Belmont, California: Wadsworth Publishing Co., 1963), pp. xix + 489.
Winfrey, Robley, *Technical and Business Report Preparation* (3rd ed.; Ames, Iowa: Iowa State University Press, 1962), pp. x + 340.

chapter 8
organizing the material

The final chapter of this book, "Coordinating the Content of the Work," primarily presents the standard form and substance of the first and last chapters of the manuscript. The subject and content of the work usually have little effect upon this standard form, but, of course, there are instances when deviation is preferable.

There is no standard form for the other chapters of the manuscript; their organization depends entirely upon the objective of the study, the abilities and interests of the student, the preference of the adviser, the data available, and other such factors. This chapter on organizing the material provides the student with background for *constructing these intermediate chapters.* This background includes both concepts of organization and the various outline forms through which these concepts can be implemented. The former will be discussed here and the latter in Chapter 9.

The most successful outlines are "developmental" in nature. It is desirable to begin with a "rough" outline, consisting of the main subject headings to be treated, arranged according to one of the systems to be described here: chronological, topical, spatial, institutional, logical, cause-and-effect, or a combination of two or more.

Then in a second outline draft each subject heading is divided into subheadings; each of the subheadings is carved into subheadings in turn. The final draft of an outline (the term "draft" is appropriate because an outline is subject to many changes before it finally becomes the table of contents of the paper) evolves from careful study of the second draft, discussions of its organization with authorities and others, and preliminary research on the entire project. The final draft will be more detailed than its predecessor and will also reflect changes in sequence and relative importance of headings from the first and second drafts.

Systems of Organization

The starting point in organizing the material is the arrangement of the note cards in an order that facilitates both logical expression of ideas and access to pertinent information. Otherwise the job of writing can be overwhelming. Several systems of organization are given here.

Chronological. In the chronological approach, the student arranges his cards in a definite *time order.* In the field of management, for example, the student's overall objective may be to trace the development of managerial practices in the United States since pre-Revolutionary days. Then he may divide his cards into separate piles according to century.

He also can set time periods based upon position levels rather than upon an objective time scale. It is well known that the successful corporation president moves through successive position levels. The cards may be divided according to the succession of those levels: junior engineer, senior engineer, engineering manager, vice-president, president.

There is no reason why a chronological system cannot be combined with some other form. Within any one century, for example, management of furniture companies can be studied according to topic: organization, training, compensation, plant location, and so on.

Topical. The topical approach is one in which the order of the cards is dictated by subjects, rather than by time. Each subject or topic becomes one unit for descriptive and analytical purposes. In the furniture example already described, the cards can be categorized so that they define a furniture manufacturer's position: construction materials, channels of distribution, organization, wage costs, and number and location of plants.

It is, of course, up to the student to judge the relative importance of topics and to deal with them in the sequence that best furthers the objectives of his work. The final sequence may be guided by considerations of analytical clarity, subjective importance, or available data.

Topical arrangements may also be combined with others. After a *topical* grouping of the cards, each deck can be further divided geographically; the plant-location topic cards can thus be subdivided by states or cities.

Spatial. The manuscript may concentrate on physical (geographical or spatial) relations. A community study may proceed on a neighborhood-by-neighborhood basis, investigating one area thoroughly before moving on to an adjacent area. In the study of the operation of a department store, spatial organization might be successful on a floor-by-floor basis, from the basement to the top. Within each floor, the spatial approach could be applied to departments.

The spatial arrangement can be combined with other systems of analysis. The cards might thus first be divided so that they deal with low-, medium-, and high-priced lines of merchandise in the department store (a *topical* arrangement, with price category as the key selector topic). Then each of these three piles of cards might be subdivided according to floor.

Institutional. The institutional approach requires separating the cards on the basis of social, business, ecological, and other types of organization. To continue with our furniture analogy, this approach would require an investigation of the operating methods, problems, costs, and other characteristics of the various component *organizations*, or institutions, of the total furniture industry, from the raw-materials producer to the consumer; the note cards would be separated so that each stack deals with only one of these components.

The institutional approach lends itself readily to combination with other categorical systems. For example, the note cards may first be separated according to raw-materials manufacturers, wholesalers, and retailers. Then each of these three stacks may be further divided topically, according to personnel requirements, costs, equipment, location, and pricing.

Logical. A logical order is one in which material is presented in steps, perhaps from the simple to the complex (as in preparing for higher mathematics by covering its simpler bases) or from the general to the particular (as when an initial broad statement like "long-range planning is not yet fully accepted by businessmen as an important area of management operations" is followed by such supporting data as the low status of long-range planning departments in the firm, small planning budgets, and so on). Of course, the latter order can also be reversed in in a particular-to-general scheme.

Cause-and-Effect. The cause-and-effect approach often takes the form of experimental work. The hypothesis is stated, the variable factor is examined and manipulated, and the effects of the manipulation are described. Assume that experiments have been conducted to determine the effects of changing materials upon the amounts of goods purchased by consumers. The note cards are separated according to the materials used (the cause); then they are further divided according to the effects of using this material: higher sales, constant sales, lower sales, and so on.

The cause-and-effect organizational system can be valuable even without an experiment. For example, one might examine the causes of several current business phenomena—the trend away from older executives, the acceleration of automation, the rise of the data-processing department or the like. The note cards would first be organized so that data on each of these "effects" was in a separate pile. Then the cards for each "effect" would be separated again according to causes.

Combined Systems. There are few subjects and treatments that lend themselves to any one system of organization so completely that there is absolutely no need for any other system. Rather, one system is usually the primary sorting tool, whereas one or more additional systems are secondary tools for organizing the note cards.

In any event, the study must be organized to fit its subject, its purpose, its audience, the skills of its writer, and the nature of the research material available. Not only must the combination of concepts fit these criteria, but all the data must also be presented in an order that leads toward some logical conclusion. This requirement should not be interpreted to mean that *everything* must be aimed at one ultimate climax; rather, individual chapters should be organized so each has its own logical conclusions.

Bibliography

Bromage, Mary, *Writing for Business* (Ann Arbor, Michigan: University of Michigan Press, 1965), pp. xii + 178.

Brooks, Cleanth, and Robert P. Warren, *Modern Rhetoric* (New York: Harcourt, Brace and World, 1958), pp. xvi + 869.

Dugdale, Kathleen, *A Manual on Writing Research* (Bloomington, Indiana: Indiana University Bookstore, 1962), p. 50.

Gorrell, Robert M., and Charles Laird, *Modern English Handbook* (3rd ed.; Englewood Cliffs, New Jersey: Prentice-Hall, Inc., 1962), pp. xxiv + 645.

Guam, Carl, Harold Graves, and Lyne Hoffman, *Report Writing* (3rd ed.; Englewood Cliffs, New Jersey: Prentice-Hall, Inc., 1950), pp. xv + 384.

Gunning, Robert, *New Guide to More Effective Writing in Business and Industry* (Boston: Industrial Education Institute, 1962), p. 332.

Koefod, Paul, *The Writing Requirements for Graduate Degrees* (Englewood Cliffs, New Jersey: Prentice-Hall, Inc., 1964), pp. xv + 268.

Lambuth, David, *The Golden Book on Writing* (New York: Viking Press, 1963), pp. xiv + 81.

chapter 9
outline systems
for the manuscript

Now that the note cards have been grouped according to a chronological, topical, or other system, two more steps remain before the writing process can begin. One is the preparation of a writing outline or "road map" from the note cards; the other, which does not fall within the purview of this book, is the analysis of the data. An outline is absolutely essential in shaping the finished manuscript. A good outline will accomplish the following:

1. Establish easily recognized structural relationships among the data and tell both the writer and the reader *how important* each piece of information is in relation to the others.

2. Show the student how the work is to be tied together into the coherent structure necessary to a good manuscript.

3. Supply useful and consistent headings and subheadings for the text.

4. Permit the student to see easily what information he has, what he needs, what is irrelevant, and where to place emphasis in research and writing.

5. Enable the student to write more easily and more quickly with less need for revison and higher-quality results.

6. Allow the reader to understand it much more readily.

Although the analogy has been made many times before, it is worth repeating that the outline is to the writer what the blueprint is to the engineer; the quality of the finished product is directly related to the completeness of the plan.

Many authorities on writing have prescribed outline systems. They generally take one of two main forms. In either instance it is of utmost importance to structure the outline so that the relative weights of the headings and their interrelations are crystal clear. How to make this structure immediately clear to the reader is discussed in detail in Chapter 15 in the section entitled "Techniques for Emphasis."

The Numerical System

This system is also called the decimal form of outlining. It depends upon the use of numbers to designate the various sections or parts of the outline, together with their relationship to each other. A specific example of this system is shown in Figure 8, while the general approach is illustrated below:

    1. Major heading (frequently a *chapter* heading)
      1.1 First-order subheading
        1.2 Second-order subheading
          1.3 Third-order subheading
            1.4 Fourth-order subheading
            Etc.
    2. Major heading (e.g., a chapter heading)
      2.11 First-order subheading (first item)
      2.12 First-order subheading (second item)
        2.2 Second-order subheading
          2.31 Third-order subheading (first item)
          2.32 Third-order subheading (second item)
            2.4 Fourth-order subheading
            Etc.

Whole numbers are used to designate major sections of a paper, chapters of a thesis, or other large divisions. When these numbers are followed by decimal points and more numbers, they refer to subsections of the major section or heading.

---

    1. Management Functions
      1.1 Planning the future course of the enterprise
        1.2 Long-range planning versus short-range planning
          1.3 Long-range planning systems
            1.41 Policies for long-range planning systems
            1.42 Procedures for long-range planning systems

    2. The Production Cycle and Planning
      2.11 Biological analogies
      2.12 Stages of the production cycle
        2.21 The introductory phase
        2.22 The growth phase
        2.23 The maturity phase
          2.31 Compensation planning in the maturity phase
          2.32 Inventory policies in the maturity phase
          2.33 Training policies in the maturity phase

Figure 8

A NUMERICAL OUTLINE SYSTEM

Figure 8 (Cont'd.)

2.41 Training by the personnel department

2.42 Training by foreman

2.43 Training by professional training consultants

   2.51 Advantages of using training consultants

   2.52 Disadvantages of using training consultants

3. Managerial Decision Making

  Etc.

The Numerical-Alphabetical System

The numerical-alphabetical system, as its name suggests, combines Roman and Arabic numerals with upper- and lower-case letters of the alphabet. For example:

  I. Major heading
    A. First-order subheading
      1. Second-order subheading
        a. Third-order subheading
          (1) Fourth-order subheading
            (a) Fifth-order subheading
    B. First-order subheading
      1. Second-order subheading
      2. Second-order subheading
  II. Major heading
    A. First-order subheading

This system, shown in Figure 9, is extremely popular and is more frequently used than is the numerical system. It does, however, have the shortcoming that the number of each heading does not by itself identify its position in the outline. For shorter works, this drawback is not too great.

I. Management Functions

  A. Planning the future course of the enterprise

    1. Long-range planning versus short-range planning

      a. Long-range planning systems

Figure 9

A NUMERICAL-ALPHABETICAL OUTLINE SYSTEM

Figure 9 (Cont'd.)

      (1) Policies for long-range planning systems

      (2) Procedures for long-range planning systems

         (a) Qualitative procedures

         (b) Quantitative procedures

   B. Organizing the enterprise

     1. Functional and authority relationships

     2. Line-and-staff authority relationships

II. The Production Cycle and Planning

   A. Biological analogies

   B. Stages of the production cycle

     1. The introductory phase

     2. The growth phase

     3. The maturity phase

       a. Compensation planning in the maturity phase

       b. Inventory policies in the maturity phase

       c. Training policies in the maturity phase

         (1) Training by the personnel department

         (2) Training by foreman

         (3) Training by professional training consultants

           (a) Advantages of using training consultants

           (b) Disadvantages of using training consultants

III. Managerial Decision Making

   Etc.

Typing from the Outline System

It almost always looks better to omit the outline numbers or letters from the final draft. If they were to be included, the work would look too mechanistic and monotonous. When they are omitted, however, the relative importance of the various parts of the manuscript must be communicated to the reader through the two remaining cues in the outline: indentation and typing (upper- or lower-case letters, underscoring, and so on). Regardless of how much indentation is used, the text that appears after each heading or subheading is carried to the left-hand margin of the paper; the exceptions are the first lines of paragraphs and some forms of quoted material. It is not good practice to put a heading on a page if the following text cannot at least be started on that same page. Figure 10 presents a useful guide for indentation and typing:

MANAGEMENT FUNCTIONS

This heading can be centered, typed in capital letters, underlined, and separated by four lines of space from the following text.

PLANNING THE FUTURE COURSE OF THE ENTERPRISE

The first-order subheading can be placed at the left margin, typed in capital letters, underscored, and separated by three lines of space from the following text.

Long-Range Planning Versus Short-Range Planning

The second-order subheading can be placed at the left margin, typed with only initial capital letters, underscored, and separated by three lines of space from the following text.

Long-Range Planning Systems

The third-order subheading can be indented one-half inch from the left margin, typed with only initial capital letters, underscored, and separated by three lines of space from the following text.

Policies for Long-Range Planning Systems. This fourth-order heading can be indented one-half inch from the left margin, typed with only initial capital letters, underscored, and terminated with a period. The following text begins on the same line as the heading, two letterspaces after the period.

Fifth-Order Subheading. This heading is the same as the fourth-order subheading, except that it is not underscored.
Note: All headings are to be typed at least three spaces below the text above them.

Figure 10

INDENTATION AND TYPOGRAPHY OF HEADINGS

Topic and Sentence Outlines

Regardless of the outline system chosen, there are two types of outline entry to choose from. In the *topic* outline headings consist simply of suggestive words or phrases. In a *sentence* outline, as the name implies, each heading or subheading is a complete sentence. This type ordinarily can be adopted only after more preliminary research has been done, whereas the topic-outline system is useful right from the beginning since it does not require as much knowledge of the subject.

Parallel Structure

Regardless of the structural or grammatical outline system that is used, parallel structure must be maintained; all subheadings at any single level of organization should take the same form, especially as the heads and subheads of the outline may be used in the paper itself. In addition, the topics of the subheadings should be mutually exclusive.

    I. Techniques of Organizing Branch Offices
        A. Organizing via centralization theories of control
        B. Decentralizing branch offices' control

This example is poor, for the two subheadings, though of the same level, refer to overlapping topic areas. A better version:

    I. Techniques of Organizing Branch Offices
        A. Centralizing branch-office control
        B. Decentralizing branch-office control

It is *possible* to use a different type of parallel structure under another *major* heading of the same manuscript, but it is not recommended. The overriding consideration is, of course, that the structure should facilitate research.

Bibliography

Anderson, Chester, Alta Saunders, and Francis Weeks, *Business Reports: Investigation and Presentation* (3rd ed.; New York: McGraw-Hill Book Co., Inc., 1957), pp. vii + 407.

Babcock, C. Merton, *The Harper Handbook of Communication Skills* (New York: Harper & Brothers, 1957), pp. xiv + 489.

Brooks, Cleanth, and Robert P. Warren, *Modern Rhetoric* (New York: Harcourt, Brace and World, 1958), pp. xvi + 869.

Gorrell, Robert M., and Charles Laird, *Modern English Handbook* (3rd ed.; Englewood Cliffs, New Jersey: Prentice-Hall, Inc., 1962), pp. xxiv + 645.

Graves Harold F., and Lyne Hoffman, *Report Writing* (4th ed.; Englewood Cliffs, New Jersey: Prentice-Hall, Inc., 1965), pp. viii + 286.

Hays, Robert, *Principles of Technical Writing* (Reading, Massachusetts: Addison-Wesley, 1965), pp. xii + 324.

Schneider, Ben, Jr., and Herbert Tjossem, *Themes and Research Papers* (New York: The Macmillan Co., 1962), pp. viii + 77.

Sherman, Theodore A., *Modern Technical Writing* (2nd ed.; Englewood Cliffs, New Jersey: Prentice-Hall, Inc., 1966), pp. xvii + 418.

Ulman, Joseph, Jr., and Jay Gould, *Technical Reporting* (New York: Henry Holt and Co., 1959), pp. vii + 382.

Williams, Cecil, and John Ball, *College Writing* (New York: Ronald Press Co., 1957), pp. xix + 475.

chapter 10
notes and footnotes

A note contains a reference, explanation, or comment outside the main body of the text. If it is placed at the bottom of a page or under a table, chart, or illustration, it is a footnote. Notes are an important part of the manuscript; you will probably have at least one on each page. Although notes serve various purposes, there are a number of generally applicable rules. This chapter specifies *precisely when and how* footnotes should be used in a thesis, dissertation, or report on a business subject.

When to Use Footnotes

To Indicate Sources of Information. Much of your information will be drawn in one form or another—quotation, paraphrase, summary, chart, table, or the like—from the works of other writers or speakers. Custom and ethics require that you acknowledge *all* sources used, regardless of how you use them. You must give credit in a note not only when you quote exactly but also when you borrow theories, ideas, or points of view and put them into your own words. When you are in doubt over whether or not you "owe" some source a footnote reference, ask yourself, "Was the idea in this source at least moderately helpful in forming my own ideas?" or "Is the fact less than common knowledge in this field?" If the answer to either question is yes, include a reference note.

When you cite the source of your information you also shift responsibility to that source. The reference tells your faculty adviser and other readers where they can check and verify your material. A scholar can judge the breadth and depth of your research simply by glancing through your notes.

To Amplify Information. Certain information that is not central to the main argument of the text may disrupt the continuity of your presentation yet be sufficiently important for inclusion in a note. For example, a description of a management-training program that has been discontinued, a minority court opinion, or an editorial aside may be conveniently placed in a note. Much other material that tends to interfere with the textual flow—derivations of equations and chemical formulas, alternative proposals, qualifications of general statements, and so on—can be placed in notes.

To Refer to Related Parts of the Work. Use footnotes for cross references.

When Not to Use Footnotes

A few words of caution are necessary lest you be carried to extremes. Your instructor does not want every sentence, paragraph, and thought footnoted; that would suggest to him that you have no ideas of your own. Every good manuscript contains the author's own ideas, perhaps based on, generated by, or tested against those of other students of the subject. The following parts of your text should *not* be credited to authorities:

1. Your ideas, opinions, conclusions, and recommendations
2. Tables, graphs, or illustrations made from data compiled by you
3. Information that is common knowledge
4. Your primary research results, for example, the tabulated results of questionnaires designed and distributed by you (but when you report the response of a specific organization you should identify the respondent in a note)

How Many Footnotes Should You Use?

How many notes to use is a frequent question, and unfortunately there is no clear-cut answer. The number depends upon many factors, among them the policy of your school, your topic, your approach, and so forth.

These *rough* rules of thumb may serve as guides, however:

1. Unless there are compelling reasons for having more or fewer (many valuable original works have relatively few footnotes), one footnote per page is a good average to aim for.
2. If you have several pages in succession without footnotes, it is likely that you have neglected to give proper credit to sources. Especially in an original study the distribution of the notes may vary, being relatively heavy in the first chapter or two, where the foundations from other work are being laid; fairly light through the middle chapters, where the original, analytical, and interpretive material appears; and then heavier when final comparisons are made.
3. Ordinarily, dependence upon a small number of sources is *not* satisfactory evidence of sufficient scholarly research and independent thinking; there are few business topics in which you cannot examine and cite at least seventy-five different sources. On the other hand, avoid using unnecessary or irrelevant notes in an effort to demonstrate a wide field of research, for such easily recognizable gimmicks defeat the purpose of the paper.

Where to Locate the Footnote Number

The footnote is itself placed at the bottom of the page (see the example at the bottom of next page) but it is called to the reader's attention by an Arabic numeral at the appropriate point in the text.[1] The number is raised about half a space above the normal line and is called a "superscript." It follows without a space any punctuation mark—period, quotation mark, parenthesis—that may be present. No punctuation mark of any kind is necessary after the superscript.

The best place for the superscript is immediately after the material to which the note refers. If this material consists of more than one sentence, then the superscript should be placed immediately after the last sentence. When different parts of a sentence have different references, each superscript must follow immediately after the part to which it refers, whether it be a single word, a phrase, or a parenthetical statement.

When to Insert the Footnotes

Insert the superscripts when you write your first draft, so that later you will not have a lot of tiresome work connecting the right sources to particular sentences.

When you type this draft, you will have to leave space for footnotes, as well. An easy way to determine how much is to insert the notes in the body of the manuscript between horizontal lines. Then the typist who prepares the second draft will know, simply by counting lines, how much space to leave at the bottom of the page.

Make sure that the footnotes are complete and in the right form. Students frequently think that they can save time by using abbreviations or ignoring proper form in the early drafts. Once abbreviations or improper forms have been adopted, however, it can be quite difficult to eliminate them.

Most schools require that notes be numbered consecutively within each chapter, though some do require that they be numbered consecutively throughout the entire manuscript. If your school or department does not specify which method to use, then it is wise to choose the former. It has two advantages: first, any need for renumbering will not require rectifying the entire work; second, if your manuscript is going to have more than one hundred footnotes, it is neater and quicker to try to stay within a two-digit system.

You can often avoid having to erase and renumber superscripts and footnote numerals by obtaining permission to insert an additional footnote (for example, you might insert "14a" after superscript "14") or to delete one (for example, if you delete note "18," you will then relabel superscript "17" so that it reads "17-18").

Each footnote must be complete the first time that it is cited in a chapter. Subsequent references to the same source can be abbreviated, according to certain conventions, within that chapter.

[1]Kurt R. Stehling, *Lasers and Their Applications* (Cleveland: World Publishing Co., 1966), pp. 214-217. Some writers prefer to employ symbols like the * (asterisk), † (dagger), § (section mark), ‖ (parallel), ¶ (paragraph mark), or other special characters like #, to designate footnotes (these symbols can also be doubled). This system is unwise because only a few symbols are available on standard typewriters, and their use can be confusing.

Where to Place Footnotes

Most colleges and universities require that footnotes be placed at the bottom of the page on which the appropriate superscripts appear (see the section of this chapter on locating notes for an example).

In typing footnotes, leave two single line spaces below the last text line on the page. Then, using underscore key, type a line about 1½ inches long (fifteen spaces on a typewriter with pica type and eighteen on one with elite type) from the left-hand margin, to separate the footnotes from the text. Skip two more line spaces. Type the superscript at the left margin, with the carriage half a space above the line. Do not put any punctuation after this numeral, and do not leave any space after it; return the carriage to normal line, and begin to type the note immediately after the superscript.

If the footnote takes more than one line, begin each subsequent line at the left-hand margin under the superscript.

Individual footnotes are single spaced, but there should be a double space between footnotes. The footnotes should, of course, be typed in numerical order.

Occasionally, it is necessary to start a footnote on a page where there is insufficient room to finish it. In such an instance, it is simply continued on the following page, separated from the text by a 1½-inch rule, as before, and preceding any footnotes that begin on that page. It is not proper to write "continued on next page" or a similar phrase at the bottom of the first page.[2]

Short footnotes with standard spacing above and below take up a great deal of room and make the page unattractive; the rules permit them to be typed on the same line, as long as three letter spaces separate them. All the footnotes must, nevertheless, be complete. You may also add a short footnote in the space following the end of a longer citation.

Multiple Footnotes

Generally, each footnote requires a separate superscript. On occasion, however, one superscript can refer to more than one reference, for example, several works by a single writer can be combined in a single large footnote, with individual references separated by semicolons.

It is preferable—for the sake of appearance and clarity—to use a separate superscript for each citation. Again, assuming that you are referring to several works by the same writer, simply separate each superscript by a comma, and do not leave spaces between them. For example, "This view has been expressed on numerous occasions in management journals by Dale.[14,15,16,17]"

Of course, some schools require that, in a case such as that just illustrated, all references be subsumed under one footnote.

[2]These three sentences are an example of a footnote that is extremely long and cannot be completed within the space available at the bottom of the page. Accordingly, it is

The Proper Form for Footnotes

We have described the functions, quantity, and placement of footnotes. Now we shall discuss the proper forms of citation for books, periodicals, pamphlets, speeches, newspapers, and any other source likely to be encountered in business research. Custom dictates that these forms *be followed exactly*.

Books

References to a book have the following form and sequence:

1. *The name of the author*, or authors. Do not abbreviate; place the first name before the last. Include any initials given on the title page; do not change the sequence of the author's names on this page. Place a comma after the last name.

> Robert I. Sarbacher, <u>Encyclopedic Dictionary of Electronics and Nuclear Engineering</u> (Englewood Cliffs, New Jersey: Prentice-Hall Inc., 1959), p. 4.

2. *The title of the book* is underlined. Capitalize the initial letter of the first word in the title and do this for all other words aside from articles, prepositions, and conjunctions.

3. *The facts of publication*, all of which are enclosed in parentheses as shown in paragraph 1 above.

> a. the edition number if there has been more than one; it should be abbreviated ("3rd ed."; "rev. ed.") and followed by a semicolon;
>
> b. the number of volumes in a multivolume work is also abbreviated ("3 vols.") and followed by a semicolon;
>
> c. the place of publication, followed by a colon;
>
> d. the name of the publisher, followed by a comma;
>
> e. the date of publication;
>
> f. a comma after the closing parenthesis around "a-e" above.

4. *The page number(s)*, followed by a period.

Some elaboration about each of the above will be presented now, and then examples of the various forms possible will be given.

The Author's Name. When more than three authors are listed on the title page, you are permitted to use only the full name of the first, followed by the abbreviation *et al.*

When the author is not given on the title page, the reference should begin with the title of the book. On the rare occasion when you know who

---

finished on the next page. Most authorities believe that, whenever possible, the writer should try to complete every footnote on a single page.

wrote the book, even though it is not revealed on the title page, you can insert the author's name if you place it within brackets.

The *author's titles or position*—Professor, Doctor, Ph.D., Personnel Manager, Buyer, and so on—are omitted.

Books that are compilations of journal articles—this is quite common in business research—are cited first under the author of the article included in the compilation and then under the name of the editor or compiler (see footnote example 7 on page 73).

Occasionally, the author is a trade association, professional society, corporation, or the like. If such an "organization" name is given instead of an individual—use it.

The Book's Title. The correct title of the book appears on the title page, not on the binding or a dust jacket. When there is a subtitle, include that in the footnote, but separate it from the main title by a colon; underscore both the title and subtitle.

The Place of Publication. The place of publication is usually found on the title page. However, many publishers also list more than one city on that page. In this case, always assume that the first city mentioned is the one to be cited. If that city is not well-known, give the state too, and separate city and state with a comma. In the case of books published in other nations, give the name of the country in addition to the city, if the latter is not well-known. When the place of publication is not specified, use the letters "n.p." in brackets.

The Publisher. This name should be fully copied from the title page. A trade or professional association, corporation, or other organization can be the publisher. When the publisher is not given, write the initials "n.n." for "no-name" in brackets. Due to widespread mergers among publishers in recent years, it has become necessary to point out that the writer must cite the exact name of the publishers of the particular reference book. Put the new, current name of the publisher in brackets after the name on the title page.

The Date of Publication. The date to be used, is that of the specific edition or revision. When no publication date appears on the title page, use the copyright date that is usually found on the page following. When that, too, is missing, put the letters "n.d." for "no date" in brackets.

When referring to a multivolume work published over a period of more than one year, cite the inclusive dates of publication: 1964-1968. When the series of volumes is not yet complete, give the date as "1968-   ."

The Page Numbers. All of the pages used in your work must be cited. A single page is referred to by a lower case "p," followed by a period: "p. 36." More than one page is referred to by two lower case "p's": "pp. 36-42."

Examples of Book Footnotes

1. Books Written by One Person.

[1] Earl P. Strong, The Management of Business: An Introduction (New York: Harper & Row, 1965), pp. 223-234.

In this example, note that the subtitle begins after the word "Business" and is also underlined.

2. Books Written by Two Authors.

[2] Herbert J. Chruden and Arthur W. Sherman, Jr., Personnel Management (Cincinnati: South-Western Publishing Co., 1963), pp. 153-156.

3. Books Written by Three Authors. This would be the same as for two authors, except that three names would precede the title.

4. Books by More Than Three Authors.

[4] Lawrence L. Bethel, *et al.*, Industrial Organization and Management (4th ed.; New York: McGraw-Hill Book Co., Inc., 1962), pp. 27-42.

There were four authors of this book—Bethel, Atwater, Stackman, and Smith.

5. Books with No Author Shown.

[5] Accountants' Encyclopedia (Englewood Cliffs, New Jersey: Prentice-Hall, Inc., 1962), pp. 123-127.

6. Books with No Author Shown; Name Supplied by You.

[6] [Instructional Staff, Commercial Trades Institute, Joseph W. Entress, Educational Director], Automatic Transmissions (New York: McGraw-Hill Book Co., Inc., 1955), pp. 370-382.

7. Edited or Compiled Works.
a. When the editors' own commentary is being cited:

[7] Carl Heyel, *et al.* (eds.), Encyclopedia of Management (New York: Reinhold Publishing Corp., 1963), pp. 331-333.

b. When part or all of an article in a collection is being cited, and it is not written by the compiler or editor but by another author, use the following:

[7] Douglas McGregor "Staff-Line Relationships", Organizational Behavior and Administration: Cases, Concepts and Research Findings, eds. Paul R. Lawrence, *et al.* (Homewood, Illinois: Dorsey Press, Inc., 1961), pp. 747-751.

Note that the author and title of the article, as well as the editors and title of the book, are given.

c. When one author's book is edited or compiled by another:

[7] Thorstein Veblen, Portable Veblen, ed. Max Lerner (New York: Viking Press, 1948), pp. 81-84.

d. When the author compiles only his own work:

[7] Peter Hicks, "The Growth Phase", Production Planning and Control (New York: Parker, Inc., 1967) pp. 222-234.

8. Translated Books.

[8] Eugenio Rignano, The Social Significance of the Inheritance Tax, 1924, trans. William John Shultz (New York: Alfred A. Knopf, Inc., 1924), pp. 16-34.

Shultz is the translator.

9. Books in Which an Organization is the Author.

[9] The United States Department of Commerce, Business and Defense Services Administration, United States Lumber Imports (Washington, D.C.: U.S. Government Printing Office, 1960), pp. 1-3.

10. a. Footnote Form for an Edition of a Book.

[10] Michael J. Jucius, Personnel Management (5th ed.; Homewood, Illinois: Richard D. Irwin, Inc., 1963), pp. 96-103.

Note that this is a fifth edition and both the words "fifth" and "edition" may be abbreviated in the footnote.

b. To present additional information about an edition, for example, to show that it is just a reprint:

[10] David Ricardo, Principles of Political Economy and Taxation, ed. E. C. K. Gonner (London, England: G. Bell and Sons, 1891), p. 47. This is a reprint of the 3rd edition which was originally published in 1821.

11. A Book by One Author as Part of a Series of Books Edited by Another Person.

[11] Saul W. Gellerman, The Management of Human Relations, Basic Management Series, eds. Huxley Madeheim, Edward Mazze, and Charles Stein (New York: Holt, Rinehart and Winston, 1966), pp. 38-41.

Note that the series title is added to the book's title and separated only by a comma.

12. Form Specifying the Volume of a Book.

[12] H. A. Antosiewicz (ed.), Proceedings of the Second Symposium in Linear Programming, vol. 2 (Washington, D.C.: National Bureau of Standards, Office of Scientific Publications, 1955), pp. 57-62.

13. Form for an Unpublished Thesis or Book.

[13] Charles G. Bryan, Research Manager's Compensation in the Petrochemical Industry (The City College, Bernard M. Baruch School of Business and Public Administration; New York: unpublished Master's Thesis, 1968), pp. 83-97.

[13] Ralph M. Brown, Marketing Systems Analysis (New York: unpublished manuscript, 1968), pp. 32-38.

Note that in each of the two examples immediately above the location is not that of the publisher—there is none—but in the first case that of the college, and in the second instance that of the author.

Examples of Report Footnotes

Footnotes used for *reports* follow as closely as possible the format detailed above for books. Examples of the several modifications occasionally necessary are given below. If you should find that still other forms are required for your purposes, the rule to follow is to adhere as closely as possible to the format for books, while giving the reader all possible information as to who sponsored the report and where it may be obtained.

14. Report by an Association—One of a Series.

[14] Analyzing and Improving Marketing Performance: Marketing Audits in Theory and Practice (Report No. 32; New York: Marketing Division, American Management Association, Inc., 1967), pp. 3-4.

15. Report by an Association—One of a Series; Author Given.

[15] J. Roger O'Meara, Employee Patent and Secrecy Agreements (Personnel Policy Study No. 199; New York: National Industrial Conference Board, Inc., 1965), p. 9.

16. Report by an Association in Compilation Form—Paper by One Author.

[16] Alfred R. Oxenfeldt, "Pricing New Products", Establishing a New-Product Program: Guides for Effective Planning and Organization (AMA Management Report No. 8; New York: Marketing Division, American Management Association, Inc., 1958), pp. 17-29.

17. Report by an Individual.

[17] Albert Bryan, <u>Management Services of Municipalities</u>, Report to The City Manager's Group (Albany, New York: The City Manager's Group, 1967), pp. 23-28.

Note that since this report is not one of a series as in footnote examples "14-16," the words "Report to The City Manager's Group" precedes the opening parenthesis.

18. Report by an Individual in a Government Agency.

[18] Frederic G. Kayser, <u>Foreign Trade Regulations of Guyana</u>, United States Department of Commerce (Washington, D.C.: U.S. Government Printing Office, October, 1966), pp. 2-4.

The title of the sponsoring agency—in this case, the United States Department of Commerce—is inserted after the name of the report.

Article Footnotes

References to periodical articles have a different form from that used for books and reports. This form is as follows:

1. *The name of the author* or authors. Do not abbreviate; place the first name before the last; follow with a comma: that is, the rules for the author's name are the same as those given above for *books*.

2. *The title of the article.* Reference to the title is different from that of a book. In the article reference, it is placed inside quote marks, with a comma after the closing quotation mark. Capitalize the initial letter of the first word in the title and all other words aside from prepositions, articles, and conjunctions. This is illustrated in example 1 on page 77.

3. *The name of the journal or magazine* is underlined. As in the title of the article, the initial letter of the first word in the journal title is capitalized together with all other words aside from prepositions, articles, and conjunctions. There is *no* punctuation mark following the title of the journal. See example 2 on page 77.

4. *The facts of publication.*

a. The *date* is enclosed in parentheses and followed with a comma; use a comma to separate the month from the year, for example (June, 1966). Do *not* use a number to designate the month, use the name only.

b. The *volume* number is followed by a comma. "Volume" is never spelled out, but is abbreviated as "Vol." and followed by the volume number, which is always in Arabic numbers, even if the original source used Roman numbers, for example, "Vol. 11."

c. The *issue* number is followed by a comma. This too, is always in Arabic numbers no matter the actual form of the journal cited. To avoid confusion with the volume number, the issue numeral is preceded by the abbreviation "No.," for example, "No. 27." Not all journals have issue numbers; when there is none, simply insert the page numbers directly after the volume number.

d. The *pages* cited are followed by a period. The same rules apply here as for book references.

Examples of Article Footnotes

1. Article Written by One Person.

[1] Charles A. Myers, "Behavioral Sciences for Personnel Managers", Harvard Business Review (July-August, 1966), Vol. 44, No. 4, pp. 154-162.

2. Article Written by Two People.

[2] Henry L. Tosi, Jr., and Robert J. House, "Management Development Beyond the Classroom", Business Horizons (Summer, 1966), Vol. 9, No. 2, pp. 91-101.

3. Article Written by Three Authors. This would be the same as for two authors, except that three names would precede the title.

4. Articles by More Than Three Authors. Instead of citing all of the authors' names, simply give the first name and follow with *et al.*, for example, Ernest Dale, *et al.* The remainder of the article footnote form is the same as for one author.

5. Articles with No Author.

[5] "Review of Current Information Pertinent to the CPI Purchasing Executive", Chemical Purchasing (May, 1966), Vol. 2, No. 4, pp. 24-25.

6. Book Review.

[6] John H. Leckenby, "Misusing Research and Development", review of Warren C. Lathrop's Management Uses of Research and Development, Management Review (March, 1965), Vol. 54, No. 3, pp. 76-77.

or:

[6] Leopold R. Mischel, review of David W. Ewing's Long Range Planning for Management, Management Science (September, 1964), Vol. 11, No. 1, pp. 210-211.

Citations for Other Types of Sources

1. Newspapers. Several forms are required.

a. When the author is known:

[1] Leonard Sloan, "Tiny Radio Introduced by G.E.", New York Times (July 5, 1966), Vol. 140, No. 39,609, p. 51, Col. 3.

Note that this form follows that for journal articles, with the single exception of listing the column in which the article starts, that is, Col. 3.

    b. When the author is not known:

[1] "Management Talent Needed in Brokerage Firms", New York Times (July 5, 1966), Vol. 140, No. 39, 609, p. 51, Col. 6.

    c. When the article is in a magazine section or special supplement, it uses the standard form for an article, for example:

[1] Andrew Hacker, "A Country Called Corporate America", The New York Times Magazine (July 3, 1966), Vol. 140, No. 37, pp. 8-9, 20, 24-25.

2. Radio and Television Programs. Here, as elsewhere, the rule to follow is to be complete enough so that others can refer to your original source. The citation for a radio or TV program will depend upon whether it was an individual show or part of a series, whether it was a local or network presentation, whether it was anonymous, or the speaker or producer was known, and so on. One such form would be:

[2] Henry Adams, producer, "Production Planning", CBC-TV network series on Management for the Small Businessman, July 15, 1966.

3. Speeches.

[3] Arnold L. Cooper, "Management Training for Shop Foremen", paper presented at the 11th World Conference of the United States Management Association, New York, Sept. 26, 1966.

If you have received a copy of the paper, and you know the specific page that you want to cite, insert the page number after the date as you would for a book or an article.

4. Personal or Telephone Interviews.

    a. When the respondent can be identified:

[4] Statement by Thomas F. O'Neil, Chairman of General Tire and Rubber Company, New York; July 5, 1967, personal interview.

If the interview had been conducted over the telephone, the last two words of the above citation would have been "telephone interview."

    b. When the respondent may not be identified, in order to preserve the confidential nature of the study:

[4] Statement by an executive of a major tire company, New York; July 5, 1967, personal interview.

[4] Statement by an executive of a major tire company to Harold D. Miller, Director of Research for Applied Management Research, Inc., Pittsburgh, Pa.; July 5, 1966, personal interview.

5. Encyclopedia Articles.

[5] Stanley F. Teele, "Marketing", Encyclopedia Americana (1965), International ed., Vol. 18, pp. 299-299h.

It is not necessary to give the place of publication, the publisher's name, or the names of the editions.

6. Legal References. This category includes the decisions by courts and government agencies like the Securities Exchange Commission and the National Labor Relations Board. Legal citations are, by custom, very brief, and vary according to their origin. Whenever possible, however, they should include the following constituents in the order presented:

a. The title of the case, underlined, and followed by a comma. The "v." for "versus" is always used and is never underlined.

b. The volume or section of the work in which the decision or act is reported; this is not followed by punctuation.

c. The title of the work in which it is reported.

d. The page number to which you are referring. When citing the entire case, act, etc., use only the number of the first page; at other times use only the first page of the case and the pages containing the cited material. Do not use "p." or "pp." There is *no* punctuation after the page numbers.

e. The date, in parentheses, is the last item in a legal citation. The closing parenthesis is followed by a period. When the jurisdiction of the court is mentioned, for example, "U.S.," "Mass.," "N.Y.," it is included in the parentheses with the date, and placed just prior to the date; the jurisdiction may be abbreviated. The abbreviation is separated from the date by a comma.

Examples of legal citations in Federal courts follow:

[6] Schwegmann Brothers, et al. v. Calvert Distillers Corporation, 341 U.S. 384, 71 S.Ct. 745 (1951).

[6] Fort Howard Paper Company v. Federal Trade Commission, 156 F.2d 899 (1946).

[6] Great Atlantic & Pacific Tea Company v. Federal Trade Commission, 106 F.2d 667 (3rd Cir., 1939).

[6] United States v. Darby, 312 U.S. 100 (1941).

[6] International Longshoremen's Union v. Arco Lumber Company, 77 F.Supp. 119 (Calif., 1959).

These examples are for government agencies:

[6] Lumbermen's Mutual Casualty Co. of Chicago, 75 NLRB 1132 (1948).

[6] Columbia River Packers Association, 44 FTC 118 (1947).

7. Statutes and Regulations. References to a statute or regulation should include its official title, date of enactment, and the section or sections that you are specifically citing:

[7] Public Law 489; An Act to Provide for the Registration and Protection of Trade-Marks Used in Commerce, to Carry Out the Provisions of Certain International Conventions, and for Other Purposes; Lanham Act: HR 1654; U.S. Statutes 1948 (79th Cong., 2d sess.) chap. 540.

[7] Public Law 717; An Act to Prohibit the Movement in Interstate Commerce of Adulterated and Misbranded Food, Drugs, Devices and Cosmetics, and for Other Purposes; S.5; U.S. Statutes 1938 (77th Cong., 3d sess.) chap. 675, sec. 403 (f).

[7] Public Law 86-257; The Labor-Management Reporting and Disclosure Act of 1959; Title 2.

[7] NLRB Rules and Regulations, Series 6, Sec. 112.9.

8. Congressional Reports. These may be of several types, for example, texts of committee hearings, preliminary reports of a Senate subcommittee, and so forth. In order to be useful, the citation should include, in the order stated: the name of the issuing committee or group, the title of the report, the branch of Congress, the number of the bill, the number and session of the Congress, the date, and the page numbers cited.

[8] Hearings before the Subcommittee on Frauds and Misrepresentations Affecting the Elderly of the Special Committee on Aging, Interstate Mail Order Land Sales, United States Senate, 88th Cong., 2d sess.; Part 41, May 18, 1964, pp. 29-43.

[8] Report of the Select Committee on Government Research, Study Number 2, Manpower for Research and Development, House of Representatives, H. Res. 504, 88th Cong., 2d sess., September 29, 1964, pp. 7-11.

9. Letters.
a. *When the writer may be identified:*

[9] Information contained in a letter from George T. Bentley, Vice-President for Personnel of Simpson Chemical Company, New York, July 7, 1966.

This form is used when the letter is sent to the author of the manuscript.

[9] Letter from George T. Bentley, Vice-President for Personnel, Simpson Chemical Company, New York to Lyndon L. Jackson, Director of Research for Applied Management Research Inc., Pittsburgh, Pa., July 7, 1966.

This form is used when the letter is sent to someone other than the author of the manuscript.

      b. When the writer may not be identified in order to preserve the confidential nature of a study:

    [9] Letter from the Vice-President for Personnel of a medium-sized chemical manufacturing company, New York, July 7, 1966.

This form is used when the letter is sent to the author of the manuscript.

      10. Reference to Materials Taken from Secondary Sources. Whenever the source that you use is not the original, then this use of secondary information ought to be mentioned in your footnote. This is important, since it will help the reader evaluate the reliability, utility, and importance of that part of your work. The general rule to follow is that the basic forms for the footnotes for books, articles, and so forth given above are to be used with the *minimum* possible modifications. You do this by fully citing the original author and source, following this by the phrase "as cited in," and then finishing by fully noting the secondary source. Examples of this follow:

      a. For a book referred to in another book:

    [10] Margaret Chandler, Management Rights and Union Interests (New York: McGraw-Hill Book Co., Inc., 1964), p. 298, as cited in Leonard R. Sayles and George Strauss, Human Behavior in Organizations (Englewood Cliffs, New Jersey: Prentice-Hall, Inc., 1966), p. 242.

      b. For an article referred to in a book:

    [10] Victor Thompson, "Hierarchy, Specialization and Organizational Conflict", Administrative Science Quarterly (May, 1961), Vol. 5, No. 4, p. 503, as cited in Leonard R. Sayles and George Strauss, Human Behavior in Organizations (Englewood Cliffs, New Jersey: Prentice-Hall, Inc., 1966), p. 288.

Subsequent References to the Source Material

      The footnote forms given so far are for *first* references to sources *in a single chapter*. For subsequent references much briefer forms, often Latin words and phrases, may be substituted; custom calls for the Latin words to be underscored.

      The guiding principle for the use of these abbreviations is to save time for the writer and the reader. A list of abbreviations is given at the end of the chapter. The three abbreviations to be discussed more fully here are all used to refer briefly to previous footnotes in a chapter.

      Ibid. If footnote references to the same work follow consecutively, there is no need to repeat the full citation, even if quite a few pages intervene between them. Of course, if *too* many pages intervene, it may be best to repeat the full footnote rather than to make the reader search for the previous reference. Use your own judgment about pages between consecutive references to the same source, but a good rule of thumb is that seven or more pages are too many.

The Latin word *ibidem*, abbreviated to *ibid.* (underlined and followed by a period) is used when the previous reference remains unchanged, except possibly for the specific page numbers cited. In the latter instance it is followed by a comma and the correct page reference. *Ibid.* can be repeated indefinitely, as long as no reference to another source breaks the sequence.

[1] Earl P. Strong, The Management of Business: An Introduction (New York: Harper & Row, 1965), pp. 223-234.

When the very next footnote is to the same text and pages, and it comes less than seven pages later, the proper citation is:

[2] Ibid.

If the subsequent footnote had been to the same text, but to different pages than the first reference, the proper citation would be:

[3] Ibid., pp. 137-142.

Op. Cit. The Latin abbreviation *op. cit.,* meaning "in the work cited," is used to refer to different pages in a work cited earlier but not immediately preceding, that is, when references to other works have intervened. The author's last name always precedes *op. cit.,* which is underscored. Note that *ibid.* can follow an *op. cit.* footnote.

[1] Earl P. Strong, The Management of Business: An Introduction (New York: Harper & Row, 1965), pp. 223-234.

[2] Charles A. Myers, "Behavioral Sciences for Personnel Managers", Harvard Business Review (July-August, 1966), Vol. 44, No. 4, pp. 155-157.

[3] Strong, op. cit., pp. 247-249.

[4] Myers, op. cit., pp. 158-161.

[5] Ibid., p. 162.

Loc. Cit. The Latin abbreviation *loc. cit.* (underscored with periods), meaning "in the place cited," is used instead of *op. cit.* when the reference is to the *exact pages* previously cited. Again the author's name must be included.

[1] Charles A. Myers, "Behavioral Sciences for Personnel Managers", Harvard Business Review (July-August, 1966), Vol. 44, No. 4, pp. 154-156.

[2] Herbert Arkin and Raymond R. Colton, Statistical Methods (New York: Barnes and Noble, Inc., 1966), pp. 101-104.

[3] Myers, loc. cit.

Caution Needed When Using Op. Cit. or Loc. Cit. Often, references are made in a single chapter to two or more works by the same author. If either *op. cit.* or *loc. cit.* were to be used in such a situation, it would not be clear which work was being cited. Consequently, instead of *op. cit.* and *loc. cit.*, a different approach must be used to briefly denote subsequent references in such cases. In fact, this new approach, which is illustrated below, may be used at *all times*, when an abbreviated footnote is called for, and not just when more than one work by the same author is at issue. This new approach is entirely acceptable, and is preferred by many students.

It is based on one simple rule: *Repeat just enough of the first reference to avoid confusion—and no more.* As with all footnote forms, page numbers are changed when appropriate:

[1] Peter F. Drucker, The Practice of Management (New York: Harper & Brothers, 1954), pp. 187-189.

[2] Drucker, Landmarks of Tomorrow (New York: Harper & Brothers, 1958), pp. 111-113.

[3] Drucker, Practice of Management, p. 102.

[4] Drucker, Landmarks of Tomorrow, pp. 117-120.

Note that subtitles can be eliminated, as there is no likelihood of confusion once the main title has been given; indeed, long titles can be abbreviated. If only the first book by Drucker had been cited and a footnote to another source had been placed after it (perhaps Myers' article from the illustration of *op. cit.*), the next reference to Drucker could have omitted even the main title of the text: "Drucker, p. 87."

Passim. The Latin word *passim*, meaning "here and there," is used to refer to various nonconsecutive pages in a book, long report, or article; it is usually appropriate in reference not to specific points but to points indicating a general approach or frequent technique:

[1] Drucker, passim.

Of course, *passim* can also be used in a full reference.

Cross References

In referring to other parts of your text, use the simplest form. For a detailed analysis of this point, see Appendix B, p. 72.

Supra, p. 57.
Cf. ante, p. 42.
Cf. post, p. 67.
Infra, p. 62.

Footnotes to Tables and Figures

Footnotes are frequently required to elaborate or in some way clarify a table or a figure. These footnotes are *not* separated from the table or figure by a horizontal line, as are text footnotes. Instead, skip just one line space after the body of the table (after the last row or horizontal rule) or figure legend, and start the footnote at the left-hand margin of the table or figure. If a footnote occupies more than one line, single-space it. Double space *between* footnotes.

Do not introduce these footnotes with either Arabic or Roman numerals, for they could cause confusion with text footnotes and especially with the numbers in the body of the table. Use superscript lower-case letters; symbols like the asterisk, dagger, section mark, parallel lines, paragraph mark; or special characters (see this chapter, note 1). The footnotes should be labeled consecutively only within a particular table or figure; do not continue the same sequence in subsequent tables or figures.

Any table or figure that is not original with you should carry an indication of its source. The source note is placed at least three line spaces below the last footnote to that table or chart and aligned with it at the left. The proper entry simply consists of the capitalized word "source," followed by a colon and then by a full footnote reference in one of the appropriate forms already described. Illustrations of the use of footnotes and source citations in tables and figures are shown in Chapters 12 and 13.

Editorial Footnotes

Occasionally it may be necessary to include in a note an explanation of some point in the manuscript or a few words about the reference that you are making. These footnotes are called "editorial footnotes." When such a digression or amplification is extensive (more than one-third of a page in single spacing), it belongs in an appendix; a cross reference to the appendix will then suffice at that point in manuscript. When discussion is briefer—and it usually will be—it can be placed at the bottom of the page in the same way as any other footnote. Several examples of such editorial footnotes follow:

[1] The dissenting decision in another case contained a first-rate analysis of the background of several similar violations of antitrust laws; see United States v. Henderson, 327 U.S. 102 (1964).

[2] A recent management text set forth very clearly the goals against which the American collective-bargaining system could be measured; see Walter B. Meigs, Advanced Accounting (New York: McGraw-Hill Book Co., Inc., 1966), pp. 395-397.

[3] It should be pointed out, however, that the majority of the respondents felt that they would have liked more time to complete questions 15-18 of the questionnaire.

Standard Abbreviations for Notes and Bibliography

anon.—anonymous

art., arts.—article, articles

Bk., Bks.—book, books

bull.—bulletin

c.—copyright

c. or *ca.* (*circa*)—approximate time; "about 1920" is written "*c.* (or *ca.*) 1920"

cf. (*confer*)—compare

cf. ante—compare preceding material

cf. post—compare subsequent material

chap. or ch., chaps. or chs.—chapter, chapters

col., cols.—column, columns

comp.—compiled

ed., eds.—editor or edition, editors

e.g. (*exempli gratia*)—for example

et al. (*et alii*)—and others

et seq. (*et sequens*)—and the following

f., ff.—and following

fig., figs.—figure, figures

ibid. (*ibidem*)—in the same place

idem—the same as before

i.e. (*id east*)—that is

il., illus.—illustration, illustrated by

infra—subsequently

l., ll.—line, lines

loc. cit. (*loco citato*)—in the place cited (*Loc. cit.* is never followed by a page
 citation. *Ibid.* or *op cit.* is used when pages are to be cited.)

ms., mss.—manuscript, manuscripts

n., nn.—note, notes (footnotes)

N.B. *(nota bene)*—note well

n.d.—no date

n.n.—no name

n.p.—no place

no pub.—no publisher

no., nos.—number, numbers

op. cit. (*opere citato*)—in the work cited

p., pp.—page, pages

par.—paragraph

passim—here and there

pp. 10 f.—page 10 and the following page

pp. 10 ff.—page 10 and the following pages

pt., pts.—part, parts

pseud.—pseudonym
q.v. (quod vide)—which see
rev.—revised, revision
sec., secs.—section, sections
ser.—series
sic—thus; inserted in brackets to indicate your awareness of an error
supra—preceding
tr., trans.—translator, translated, translation
v. or vol., vols.—volume, volumes
v.—versus

chapter 11
using quotations

The information that you obtain for your manuscript may be paraphrased, summarized, integrated with your own thoughts, or quoted verbatim. No exact length limit can be set for quotations, but they should be few and far between. The selections depend upon the nature of your work and the quotations themselves. Too many quotations suggest that you have not properly digested your research material and cannot put it into your own words. The relevant thoughts of others should be integrated with your own; of course, proper credit must be given at all times, either in the text or in a footnote.

Keep in mind that the purpose of a quotation is to *illustrate*, not to carry the burden of proof of what you are trying to do. After all, it is in the main body of your manuscript that you express your ideas, arguments, conclusions—*in your own words.* They provide the basis and continuity of your work. Merely pasting quotations together with connective phrases would result in an amorphous mass of words, rather than a logical exposition of your theme. There are times, though, when you *should* use extracts from other work. The requirements for doing this are presented below. These requirements apply only to quoted material; that which you paraphrase or summarize need only be denoted by a footnote.

What Should Be Quoted

It is permissible to quote from sources that are universally recognized as unique and not to be improved upon. Selections from the Bible, quotations from Abraham Lincoln or Winston Churchill, a brilliant epigram or characteristic expression all fall into this category.

> Nothing may seem simpler or more obvious than to answer what a company's business is. A steel mill makes steel, a railroad runs trains to carry freight and passengers, an insurance company underwrites fire risks. Indeed the question looks so simple that it is seldom raised; the answer seems so obvious that it is seldom given.
>
> Actually "what is our business" is almost always a difficult question which can be answered only after hard thinking and studying. And the right answer is usually anything but obvious.
>
> Peter F. Drucker, *The Practice of Management* (New York: Harper & Brothers, 1954) p. 49

Court decisions are quoted because the exact text of the decision may be crucial; interpretation may inadvertently distort the opinion of the court; the text of a bill or law usually should be quoted exactly. Policies or rules of an organization or business firm should be quoted to ensure consistency. Titles of publications, lectures, and manuscripts are cited exactly without modification or embellishment. Statistical material, that could not logically be presented in another form, may be quoted. Material may be quoted to permit comparison of style, concept, or some other feature.

Length of Quotations

Quotations should be short and to the point: generally less than one-half page of single-spaced typing each. Several difficulties may arise with longer quotations: they can interfere with continuity, contain much irrelevant material, and seem to shift authorship from you to your source. If you must have long quotations, try to place them in an appendix.

When quotations occupy more than four typewritten lines, they should be "extracted," indented one-half inch from the regular left-hand margin (on the left side of the page only), single-spaced, and without quotation marks. There should be double spaces between paragraphs of quoted material. Indent each quoted paragraph one-half inch, that is, one inch from the regular margin. If you omit the first part of the quoted paragraph begin it with an ellipsis (see next section).

Quotations of four or fewer lines should be typed as part of the text, with quotation marks. There is one exception to this "four-line rule," and it applies to quotations of four lines or less that require special emphasis. These exceptions may be indented one-half inch from your regular left-hand type margin, single-spaced, and typed without quote marks.

Presentation of Quotations

Short quotations are enclosed by quotations marks: "A sample of two hundred middle managers was used for the wage survey."

To indicate omission of material from a quoted source insert an ellipsis (three dots): "A sample . . . was used for the market survey."

If you integrate part of a quoted sentence into your own sentence, in a complete grammatical unit, you may omit the ellipsis. If the original source read, "It is often true that many product lines are too extensive for their manufacturers," you might quote it, "A leading spokesman for the industry wrote that 'many product lines are too extensive for their manufacturers.' "

Ellipses are considered part of the quotation; therefore, they are placed inside quotation marks. "One writer's comment indicated, '. . . many product lines are too extensive . . . ,' and that their manufacturers would be better off without them." In this sentence the quotation was not integrated—instead a comma was used after the fourth word—and the initial ellipsis could therefore not be eliminated. When the ellipsis comes at the end of a sentence, simply add a period before the three periods of the ellipsis.

Quotations should be reproduced exactly as printed in the original source. Changes in italics or punctuation undermine the accuracy of a quotation, and even a change in capitalization, paragraphing, or spelling may distort the author's intent.

Words may be added to a quote if necessary, but they must be placed in brackets [in 1966], [our], [at the time]. Generally words are added only for purposes of clarification. The use of brackets, rather than parentheses, is a widespread convention. If you were to use parentheses your readers might think they had been present in the original source.

There are two exceptions to the rule against changing capitalization in a quotation. Let us assume that you want to quote from this sentence: "A Department of Commerce analysis indicated that the production of automobiles in Europe was extremely good." If you write, "Among other reports, 'The production of automobiles . . . was extremely good,' " without integrating the quotation into your sentence, it is necessary to capitalize "the."

The other exception is, of course, when you *start* a sentence with a quotation: " 'The production of automobiles in Europe was extremely good,' according to a report by the United States government." Once again, "the" is capitalized.

If there is an error in the original material and you want to show that you recognize it, place the underscored Latin word *sic*, which means "so" or "thus," in brackets immediately after the error. *Sic* should be underlined and in brackets. *Sic* is also used after an astonishing quoted statement to indicate that the quotation is a literal transcription.

When you wish to underscore something in the original for emphasis, you have three alternatives: to add "emphasis mine" in brackets immediately after the emphasized material, to add it at the end of the quotation, or to put it in the footnote for that quotation. (The superscript for that footnote should go at the end of the quoted material.)

Occasionally, a quotation appears within a quotation. Then single quotation marks are used ('. . .') to enclose the inner quotation, in contrast to the double marks generally employed (". . .").

When you omit a paragraph or more from a quotation, indicate the omission by five centered periods, instead of an ellipsis.

A comma or period must *always* be placed inside the quotation marks: " 'The production,' the author stated, 'is far from satisfactory.' " Other punctuation marks are placed within the quotation marks if they were part of the original sentence. But if you are adding an exclamation mark or a question mark, it must go *outside* the quotation marks.

Quotation marks are also commonly used to highlight words or phrases used in an unusual way, not as normally understood. Slang, colloquialisms, misnomers, and technical terms are at times enclosed in quotation marks.

Authority to Quote

There are no precise rules or laws on what may be quoted without permission of the author or publisher. If only a few lines are quoted and the source credited, litigation is obviously highly unlikely. Much depends upon the nature of the material quoted. When a more elaborate quotation is essential, permission should be requested.

There is generally no cost if the source is credited. For an academic treatise not intended for sale, it is unnecessary to secure permission for quotations. If part or all of the manuscript containing a substantial quotation is sold, the faculty advisor should be consulted about obtaining permission. Every quotation from a single source should be included in a request for permission to quote from that source.

Publishers freely grant permission to quote because quotations help to publicize the works of their authors and their firms and to provide good public relations. Authors buy and recommend books from other publishers; granting permission for reasonable quotation is a reciprocal policy in most of the publishing industry.

University presses permit quotation of 1,000 words without permission; most commercial book publishers allow up to 350 words. When a publisher grants permission, it usually requests that the citation be made in a particular form. All members of the Association of American University Presses except the American branches of the Oxford and Cambridge University Presses subscribe to the "Reciprocal Agreement on Permission to Quote":

> 1. Each party to this agreement agrees to permit the other parties to quote from the originating publisher's books *without seeking specific permission* subject to the conditions listed below. 2. Full credit will be given to book, author, and publisher (and series and translator, if any). 3. Waiver of the requirement for specific written permission does not extend to verse, to illustration, to quotations totaling more than 1,000 words from any one book, or to quotations that are complete units in themselves (as brief short stories or essays). 4. It is clearly understood that this agreement applies only to quotations used for purposes of illustration or the citing of authority and not to quotations presented as primary material for its own sake (as in anthologies or books of readings). The responsibility for determining the nature of the use rests with the quoting publisher.

To obtain permission to quote, write to the permissions department of the publisher from whose publication you want to reproduce. Tell him precisely the material that you want to copy (including page numbers), how you propose to use it, how many copies you plan to make, who will see it, whether or not your work is planned as a profit-making venture, and so on.

Quotations in Appendixes and Notes

Although an interpretation or a brief quotation from a work may be offered in your text, you may also want to quote it in full or at length in an appendix. Whereas a phrase or a paragraph from a U.S. Supreme Court decision may be extracted, the entire decision should be presented in an appendix and simply noted in the text.

Quotations in notes follow the same rules as do quotations in the text.

Bibliography

Babcock, C. Merton, *The Harper Handbook of Communication Skills* (New York: Harper & Brothers, 1957), pp. xiv + 489.

Brooks, Cleanth, and Robert P. Warren, *Modern Rhetoric* (New York: Harcourt, Brace and World, 1958), pp. xvi + 869.

Hay, Robert D., *Written Communications for Business Administrators* (New York: Holt, Rinehart and Winston, 1965), pp. xix + 487.

Lambuth, David, *The Golden Book on Writing* (New York: Viking Press, 1963), pp. xiv + 81.

Sherman, Theodore A., *Modern Technical Writing* (2nd ed.; Englewood Cliffs, New Jersey: Prentice-Hall, Inc., 1966), pp. xvii + 418.

Williams, Cecil, and John Ball, *College Writing* (New York: Ronald Press Co., 1957), pp. xix + 475.

Winfrey, Robley, *Technical and Business Report Preparation* (3rd ed.; Ames, Iowa: Iowa State University Press, 1962), pp. x + 340.

chapter 12
tables

The information that you collect will frequently be statistical. Such data must be assembled, classified, and presented so that they can be quickly and clearly understood. A *table* is frequently the ideal way to present such information, for its systematic arrangement of numerical data in columns and rows permits immediate comparison, analysis, and reference. A good table needs no supplementary textual explanation.

This chapter is devoted to an explanation of the characteristics of tables and the techniques of their construction.

Types of Tables

Tables can be classified as *informal* and *formal*. The latter category is complex, but informal tables are quite simple and can easily be illustrated.

An *informal* table presents a very brief and simple set of facts that would be less understandable in verbal presentation in sentence form. These facts do not require the precise structure of a table number, title, and so on. Informal tables can often be woven into the text.

For example:

Investigation of attitudes toward the educational background of management trainees found two principal viewpoints commonplace among business executives. These views depended upon the educational background of the executives themselves. When divided into two groups, "business school graduates" and "graduates of other schools," these respondents had the following opinions about whether those hired as management trainees must be graduates of business schools:

Business School Graduates	Graduates of Other Schools
72% said essential	8% said essential
14% said desirable	10% said desirable
8% said not necessary	52% said not necessary
6% said undesirable	30% said undesirable

Another example comes from the 1966 Annual Report of the New York Central Railroad, page 24:

Consolidated debt of the entire Central System increased by $32,288,753, reflecting the $50,923,720 debt of the Strick Corporation, which was not a part of the Central System in 1965. Excluding the addition of this new company, System debt was reduced by $18,634,967 during 1966.

A summary of changes in consolidated debt since 1957 follows:

New York Central and lease lines:	December 31 1957	1966	Increase (Decrease)
Bonds	$ 701,975,100	$591,538,075	$(110,437,025)
Equipment obligations	251,456,513	120,350,448	(131,106,065)
Miscellaneous	27,219,405	17,635,728	(9,583,677)
	980,651,018	729,524,251	(251,126,767)
Strick companies[a]		50,923,720	50,923,720
Other subsidiaries	99,216,160	74,147,124	(25,069,036)
	$1,079,867,178	$854,595,095	$(225,272,083)

[a]Excluding Strick Finance Company.

In simple special-purpose tables like this one, it is permissible to round off numbers.

When more complex statistics must be presented, a *formal* table is necessary. When information seems too extensive or complex for a single table, divide it between two or more tables. The remainder of this chapter is devoted to the general principles of constructing formal tables. So many kinds of tables are possible that it is not feasible to illustrate more than a few.

Where to Place the Table

Include no table to which you do not refer in your text: if data are important enough to be included at all, they will have some function in your argument. The logical place to put a table is as close as possible to the first reference to it. A table less than half a page long can be typed right on the text page following the paragraph in which it is discussed; otherwise it should appear on the page immediately following. If the description of a full-page table must be continued to a subsequent page, the table is inserted between the beginning and end of that discussion.

Tables less than one-half page in length require some judgment in placement. Ordinarily a table does not look well sandwiched between expository matter on a page. Yet if it appears near the top of the page, there is often room below it to start a new paragraph of text. You must use judgment. If the space below the table is not great, it may be left blank, but more than a quarter-page of blank space is likely to look awkward. If less than a quarter-page would be occupied by text material, on the other hand, it is better to put the table on a separate page. Sometimes it is necessary to bend placement rules a bit. In order to place a table lower on the page, for example, it may be necessary to begin new, unrelated text material before the table.

One inviolate rule of placement is never to start a table of page length or less on one page and continue it to another. If a table is longer than one page no text should appear with it, even if the continuation takes up only a fraction of a page.

Discussion of the Table

Every formal table must be numbered and cited by number in your text. How detailed should the reference to a table be? The answer really depends upon the use of the data that you want to make. You may want to analyze the table carefully, draw conclusions from it, base theories on its data, select certain data for consideration, and so on. When you plan extended discussion of a table it is wise to number each column in parentheses above the column heading. Then, you can refer easily to the column numbers rather than to the more cumbersome word headings.

Large Tables

Often a table will be either too long or too wide to fit the margin requirements of the usual size 8 1/2 × 11 inch page. There are several ways that you can accommodate this large size.

1. For example, it is permissible to exceed the standard margin requirements for a thesis page (1 1/2 inches at the left and top, 1 1/4 inches at the bottom, and 1 inch at the right) when necessary to include a table that is slightly too long or wide. As the thesis must be bound at the left margin, the latter cannot be reduced to less than 1 inch; the others can be reduced to 1/2 inch. Be sure, however, to check with your adviser for permission to make any margin adjustments.

2. It is also permissible to use a typewriter with elite type for tables, even though the text is typed on a pica machine.

3. Another solution is to type the table on a larger sheet and then to reduce it photographically to 8 1/2 × 11 inches, as long as the data are still legible.

4. The table can also be typed on a larger sheet and folded to 8 1/2 × 11 inches. Be sure to allow, in folding, for the binding edge of the thesis.

5. When a table fits the standard width but is too long for the 11-inch sheet, it is often easiest to continue it on a second page. Be sure to repeat the table number, title, and column headings on the next page; at the bottom of the continued page be sure to include a line like "Table 14 continued."

6. When a table is too wide to fit comfortably on an 8 1/2-inch sheet, it can sometimes be turned broadside, with the title on the side that is to be bound, provided, of course, that the 11-inch dimension is sufficient for the width and that the 8 1/2-inch dimension can accommodate the length.

Numbering Pages and Tables

Page Numbers. Every page in the manuscript, including those with tables, must be numbered in sequence. Every page of a table will thus be numbered, but a folded sheet will have only one number. Regardless of the table's position (vertical or broadside) or of a fold, the page number must be placed in the upper right-hand corner (when the page is in its normal position). The page number will thus be on the *back* of a folded table page; it is a good idea to repeat the page number on the upper right-hand corner of the face of the table page.

Table Numbers. Each formal table must also be numbered as it appears, starting with Arabic numeral 1 and continuing sequentially through the end of the work. Do not begin with Table 1 in each new chapter. Each numeral should be preceded by the capitalized word "table": "Table 1," "Table 27," and so on. This label should be centered on the page.

Handling the Table Title

Every numbered table must also have a title, typed in capitals two line spaces below the table number and centered on the page. The title often requires more than one line, and these lines should be single-spaced. It usually looks better to type succeeding lines in an inverted-pyramid form, that is, to indent the second line more than the first on both sides, the third more than the second, and so on. There should be no period after the title.

The title must explain the table, giving a general idea of the subject covered, the area from which the data have been drawn, and the period of time covered. But—just as important—it should be as brief as possible without sacrificing completeness, clarity, or accuracy. When long titles are required, it is often best to relegate some of the necessary information to subtitles. The sample tables in this chapter illustrate these principles.

Whatever form you choose, be consistent throughout your manuscript.

Components of the Tables

Constructing tables is similar to constructing anything else: you must know what components are available and how they can be put together. The most common components of a table are listed here (see Tables 2-6). Variations do occur, but their use must be fully justified by the particular purpose for which the table is designed.

Table 2 ——→ Table Number

THIS IS A MODEL TABLE ←—— Title

Parts of Formal Tables, Their Designation and Arrangement ——→ Subtitle or Headnote

Multiple Column Heading

←———— Body ————→

Column Identification ——→ (1) Stubhead, (2) Column Head

Stubhead	Caption A			Caption B		
	(2) Column Head	(3) Column Head	(4) Column Head	(5) Column Head	(6) Column Head	(7) Column Head
Stub Data (Independent variables are put in the stub column whenever possible)	Dependent variables are put in the columns whenever possible. Row 4 Row 5	Row 4[a] Row 5 ← Footnote Symbol	Cell [Row 4] Row 5	Row 1 Row 2 Row 3 Row 4 [Row 5] ← Cell	Row 1 Row 2 Row 3 Row 4 Row 5[b] ← Footnote Symbol	Row 1 Row 2 Row 3 Row 4 Row 5
Totals	Column Total	Column Total				

Body

Stub

Row Identification
1
2
3
4
5
6
7
8
9
10
11

[a] Footnote a would start here.
[b] Footnote b would start here.

Source: The full citation must be given; use the same form you would for a book, article, etc.

Row. A horizontal typed line of material within a table is a row. Rows can often be arranged in groups separated by extra line space. Interpretation of monthly data can be facilitated by grouping in quarterly or semiannual blocks, separated by extra line space.

Column. A column is a vertical typed line of material within a table.

Headnote. The headnote provides more information about the nature of the title; in essence it is a subheading. Thus, if the title was "POLY-ETHYLENE PRODUCTION IN 1968," a headnote might go on to say: "New England States."

Stub. The stub is usually the first column on the left-hand side. The independent variable is usually put in the stub. Only the first word of each entry and proper nouns are capitalized.

Stub Head. The stub head is the caption for the stub, or first column. All major words are capitalized.

Body. The body of the table is all the columns to the right of the stub. Any point in the body can be located by specifying column and row.

Column Head. The heading of each column in the body identifies the data contained in the column. The heading should be as brief and precise as possible. Abbreviations are entirely acceptable. If there is a "miscellaneous" column, it should be placed at the far right of the table, just before the "totals" column, if there is one. The type of column head should be consistent within each table and among all tables in the work. All major words should be capitalized.

Caption. A caption is a heading under which column heads are grouped. If it is longer than one line it should be single-spaced.

Footnote. Footnotes are used to amplify, qualify, or comment upon the data in any part of the table. See "Footnotes to Tables and Figures" in Chapter 10.

Source Note. The source note is placed at the bottom of the table below the footnotes, if any. See "Footnotes to Tables and Figures" in Chapter 10.

Planning the Table

Arranging the Space. You can save time by apportioning space before constructing the table. The following factors must be taken into consideration:

1. The size of the paper and the desired margins, both horizontal and vertical

2. The length of the longest word, phrase, or number in the stub head and each column head

3. The length of the longest set of data in each column

4. The length of the table as determined by the number of rows

5. The width of the table as determined by the number of columns and the width of each

It is extremely important to study tables in leading business texts for examples of how they can be handled.

Arranging the Data. Careful arrangement of the data in a table is also important, to permit proper emphasis on appropriate groups of data and to facilitate analysis and comparison. Table columms are generally arranged so that data to be compared are placed next to one another. The table should contain the minimum possible number of columns.

Data should read from top to bottom in each column and from left to right in each row. A number of schemes is possible: alphabetical, geographical, chronological, conventional, and so forth.

The most common arrangement in special-purpose tables (designed to highlight certain facts) is chronological. The earliest date is in the left-hand column of the table body and at the top of the stub. Where the most recent period is of unusual interest, however, as when the figures are published for the first time, the latest figure may be listed before any of the others. In this case, it may be separated from them by a heavy or double line. Chronological presentation of data is shown in Table 3.

An arrangement of items according to their magnitude or size is commonly used. In this instance, common practice dictates that the largest figure appear at the top of the column and the others be arranged in order of size. The presentation of data by size is shown in Table 4.

Many types of data are conventionally arranged without regard to series: for example, under the headings, "men," "women," and "children" in that order.

Ruling and Spacing the Tables

In order that a table may be used effectively, it should have rules that serve to guide the eye. There are no firm requirements for either rules or spacing within the tables. You should construct the simplest table that you can, consistent with easy understanding.

Experience has shown, however, that it is often useful to rule tables in the following way:

1. Use a double horizontal line to separate the title or subtitle of the table from the stub head and captions.

2. Use a single horizontal line to separate the captions from the column heads, the column heads from the body of the table, the body from the

Table 3

IMPORTS—VALUE OF SELECTED COMMODITIES: 1921-1960
(In Millions of Dollars)

Yearly Average or Year	Hides and skins	Furs, and manu- factures	Fruits and nuts	Vegetable oils and fats, expressed or extracted	Coffee	Sugar	Rubber, crude	Tobacco, unmanu- factured	Cotton manu- factures[a]	Burlaps
1921–1925	93	81	75	60	206	295	193	65	87	60
1926–1930	118	115	85	82	282	207	294	57	64	72
1931–1935	40	43	48	45	141	113	75	27	34	26
1936–1940	51	70	60	73	138	130	206	34	42	36
1941–1945	68	108	63	44	266	172	149	50	19	50
1946–1950	92	149	151	95	732	335	311	81	52	102
1951–1955	75	85	180	90	1,410	411	493	83	88	90
1956–1960	65	96	206	93	1,217	484	340	104	186	85

[a]Includes fur hats.

Source: Statistical Abstract of the United States: 1961 U.S. Department of Commerce (82nd ed.; Washington, D.C.: Government Printing Office, 1961), p. 886.

footnotes, and the column data from column totals if the latter are included.

3. Vertical rules are unnecessary if you have only two columns. Some publications always omit vertical rules. In typewritten tables they are not essential, although it is good practice to separate the columns with single vertical lines, which can be drawn in black ink or by inserting the paper sideways in the typewriter and pressing the underscore key to make a continuous line.

4. The columns under a single caption should be separated by a single vertical line from the columns under each neighboring caption.

Table 4

USERS OF MANAGEMENT TRAINING FILMS
RESULTS OF A MAIL STUDY

Total Number of Employees	Per Cent of Respondents
Above 15,000	24%
10,000—14,999	17
5,000—9,999	7
1,000—4,999	6
500—999	5
200—499	4
unknown	37[a]
Total	100%

[a]This large response for "unknown" is probably due to the fact that the questionnaires were answered by someone other than the purchaser of the management training films.

The spacing of the table rows depends upon their number and the type of material in the table; either single or double spacing may be appropriate. In longer tables when space limitations require single spacing between rows, it is often helpful to group the rows. For example, when data are presented chronologically, a single line space can be inserted at five- or ten-year intervals.

Alignment of Data in Columns

All the figures in a column should be aligned according to their numerical and decimal values. When there are many numbers with different levels of decimal values (for example, 0.05, 0.0023, 312.47, and so on), perfect decimal alignment may require too much space. Then it is permissible to align the material without regard to decimal value.

Table 5

COMPARISON OF PRODUCTION IN TWO PLANTS

Plant Manager	Production Goal: Annual Output (in pounds)	Change in Annual Production of Company Product (in million pounds)[a]		
		1964	1965	Change
A	96,000,000	4.5	5.6	+1.1
B	102,000,000	3.1	4.3	+1.2

[a]Note that this caption applies to three columns.

Source: Adapted from Richard Barr, "Criteria for Rating Production Efficiency", Management Review (September, 1968), Vol. 55, No. 9, p. 84.

When Data Are Missing. You can indicate missing data by three techniques. In order of preference they are, typing "n.a." (for "not available"), three dots (. . .), or three hyphens (---) where the data would otherwise be inserted.

Units of Measurement. The units of measurement should always be indicated in either the captions or the column heads. If the caption is "Production Share," the column heads should specify the units of production share, for example, percentage points, units of production volume, dollars, industry rank, or the like. Including this information (using symbols like the dollar and percent signs whenever possible) in the column heads means that they do not have to be repeated with each datum in the column itself.

Totals. Totals should be separated from the remainders of the columns with single horizontal lines. Symbols like dollar or percent signs should be typed in the totals even though they appear in the columns heads. If rows are totaled, then the right-hand column will consist of these row totals.

The Table Footnotes and Source

Footnotes to a table are frequently used to provide additional information pertaining to data in the table. Full details as to their form and position in the table are presented in Chapter 10. Bear in mind, however, that when applied to tables, a footnote is defined differently than when applied to the expository part of your text. A *table* footnote merely permits you to add to the data in the table anything *but* the citation of its source.

The part of the table called "Source" is the section that contains the full citation of the origin of the data reproduced in the table; this citation uses

Table 6

INCOME OF OFFICE MANAGERS
BY AGE AND EDUCATION

Age at Nearest Birthday (in years)	High School, No College		College Graduates		Total No. of Respondents
	Mean Income (in dollars)	No. of Respondents	Mean Income (in dollars)	No. of Respondents	
25	$ 5,009	32	$ 5,842	27	59
26	5,342	27	6,431	35	62
27	6,172	42	7,204	26	68
28	6,428	21	8,139	42	63
29	7,109	39	9,024	6	45
30	7,562	17	9,782	31	48
31	8,429	7	10,784	47	54
32	8,988	40	11,492	29	69
33	9,723	36	12,277	24	60
34	11,422	33	13,481	34	67
Total	—	294	—	301	595

the same forms illustrated in Chapter 10. In order to lend authority to the data and enable the reader to seek the original source if further information is desired, it is absolutely essential to give very specific information. The source is placed immediately beneath the table and below any footnotes to the table to the left. Chapter 10 presents specific data as to the form and content of a table source note.

Bibliography

Blickle, Margaret, and Kenneth Houp, *Reports for Science and Industry* (New York: Henry Holt and Co., 1958), pp. x + 320.

Comer, David, III, and Ralph Spillman, *Modern Technical and Industrial Reports* (New York: G. P. Putnam's Sons, 1962), pp. xix + 425.

Graves, Harold F., and Lyne Hoffman, *Report Writing* (4th ed.; Englewood Cliffs, New Jersey: Prentice-Hall, Inc., 1965), pp. viii + 286.

Hay, Robert, *Written Communications for Business Administrators* (New York: Holt, Rinehart and Winston, 1965), pp. xix + 487.

Menzel, Donald, H., Howard Jones, and Lyle Boyd, *Writing a Technical Paper* (New York: McGraw-Hill Book Co., Inc., 1961), pp. ix + 132.

Sherman, Theodore, A., *Modern Technical Writing* (2nd ed.; Englewood Cliffs, New Jersey: Prentice-Hall, Inc., 1966), pp. xvii + 418.

Ulman, Joseph, Jr., and Jay Gould, *Technical Reporting* (New York: Henry Holt and Co., 1959), pp. vii + 382.

Wanous, S. J., *Statistical Typing* (Cincinnati: South-Western Publishing Co., 1956), p. 62.

Winfrey, Robley, *Technical and Business Report Preparation* (3rd ed.; Ames, Iowa: Iowa State University Press, 1962), pp. x + 340.

chapter 13
constructing graphs
and illustrations

Graphs and illustrative materials may add to the completeness and clarity of a treatise. At one time the prevalent view was that such visual aids were to *supplement* the written text, but now they often form an important part of the manuscript in their own right; more and more they are supplanting written material.

If graphs and illustrations are clear, well prepared, and informative, they can be extremely useful, but confusing, sloppy, and incomplete illustrations detract materially from the value of a manuscript. It is therefore necessary to plan them with great care.

Because the diversity of possible illustrative forms is so great, only a limited number of examples can be presented in this chapter. Before selecting those most appropriate to your manuscript, it may be fruitful to examine texts in economics, finance, management, marketing, engineering, and statistical methods and graphs. You will obtain from them insight into the most appropriate style of illustration.

Illustrations and Graphs

It is useful to distinguish briefly among the major forms of illustrations and graphs. Custom generally calls for either form to be labeled "Figure" in the thesis. Illustrations comprise a broad variety of visual aids that can make the study clearer and more attractive; frequently used types include diagrams, forms (questionnaire blanks, for example), photographs, and maps. Graphs are pictorial presentations of *statistical* data, showing exact relationships among variables. Some of the more common types of graphs are the line graph, the bar graph, and the area diagram.

Line Graphs. The line or curve graph is distinguished by the fact that the variations in the data are indicated by means of a line or a curve. It is by far the most commonly used form of graphic presentation. Generally two related variables are shown; the independent variable is placed along the x (horizontal) axis and the dependent variable along the y (vertical) axis. A line is then drawn connecting the points. A detailed dissection of a graph, showing all its components, is illustrated in Figure 11.

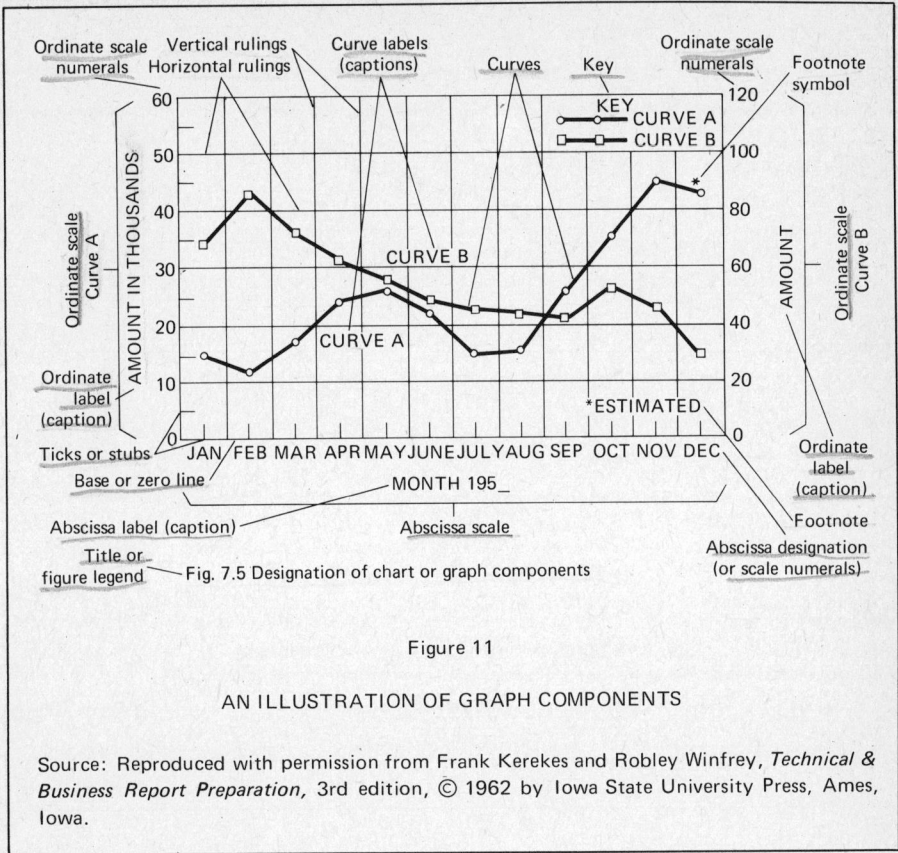

Fig. 7.5 Designation of chart or graph components

Figure 11

AN ILLUSTRATION OF GRAPH COMPONENTS

Source: Reproduced with permission from Frank Kerekes and Robley Winfrey, *Technical & Business Report Preparation,* 3rd edition, © 1962 by Iowa State University Press, Ames, Iowa.

Line graphs may be classified according to the scale used on the *x* and *y* axes: arithmetic, logarithmic, and so on.

1. On *arithmetic graphs* equal quantities of a variable are represented by equal distances between the grid lines (see Figure 12). In a *high-low graph* fluctuations of the data are presented as simultaneous fluctuations of peaks and lows. For example, in Figure 13 the highest stock price and the lowest are plotted for each trading day in a specific period. The low point and the high point for each day are connected by a heavy vertical line. These closely spaced vertical lines tend to present the eye with an irregular band, or "curve."

2. *Logarithmic and semilogarithmic graphs* are used to show relationships between variables, one or both of which is changing exponentially. In the instance of one such variable, the appropriate axis is scaled proportionally (a semilogarithmic graph). When there are two such variables both axes are marked in that way (a logarithmic graph). When the *percentage* change between two pairs of figures is constant, the differences between their logarithms will thus be equal; what would be a curved line on an arithmetic graph is converted into a straight, or at least more nearly straight, line (see Figure 14).

Net Sales

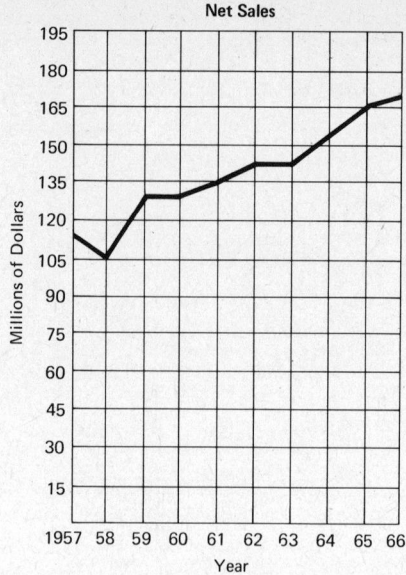

Year

Figure 12

AN ARITHMETIC LINE GRAPH SHOWING THE
GROWTH IN SALES OF THE RAYONIER CORPORATION,
1957-1966

Source: Reproduced with permission from *Annual Report, 1966* (New York: The Rayonier Corporation, 1967), p. 5.

3. A *silhouette chart* is a line graph showing positive and negative deviations from a zero or base line, with the area between the zero base line and the resulting curve filled in.

4. A *histogram,* also known as a "rectangular frequency polygon," reflects the frequency distribution of the data under consideration. Rectangles, or bars, are drawn with the width as the size of the class interval and the height as the frequency in each class interval (see Figure 15). Often, a series of lines is drawn to connect the midpoints of the bar tops.

Bar Graphs. As its name implies, the bar graph represents data in bars of varying lengths but *uniform* width. This can be seen in Figure 16. A variation is the subdivided percentage bar chart, in which a single bar represents 100 percent of some parameter, for example, expenditures; it is then divided into segments proportional to the percentages of data in each subcategory, as in Figure 17.

Bar charts may also be constructed in more pictorial form. Identical pictures of different sizes may be used for comparative purposes. To represent the gold holdings of the U.S. Treasury at different period, stacks of coins of varying heights corresponding to the varying values may be used.

In a loss-and-gain chart the bars extend from a zero line that bisects the chart horizontally or vertically. The bars to one side of the zero line represent losses, for example, and those to the other side, profits.

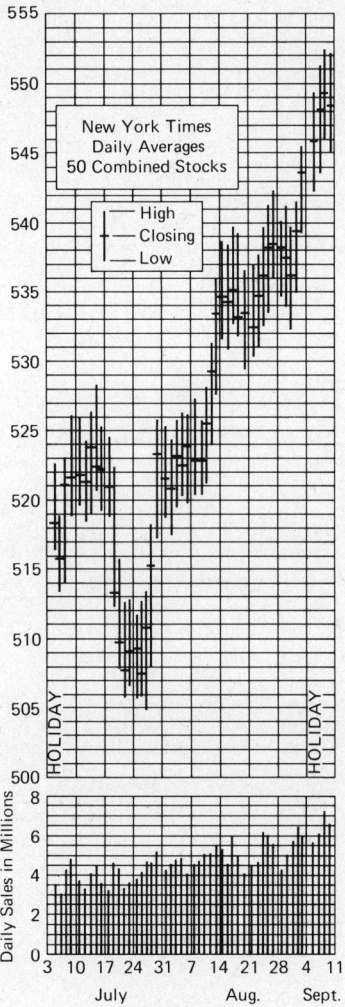

FRIDAY, SEPT. 10, 1965

Day's
Sales
6,651,540

Thursday
7,360,000

Year Ago
5,636,900

Year to Date

| | 1965 | 1964 |
| | 942,649,364 | 855,771,453 |

New York Times
Daily Averages
50 Combined Stocks

High
Closing
Low

HOLIDAY

HOLIDAY

Daily Sales in Millions

3 10 17 24 31 7 14 21 28 4 11

July   Aug.   Sept.

Figure 13

A SAMPLE OF A HIGH-LOW GRAPH
SHOWING STOCK PRICE AVERAGES

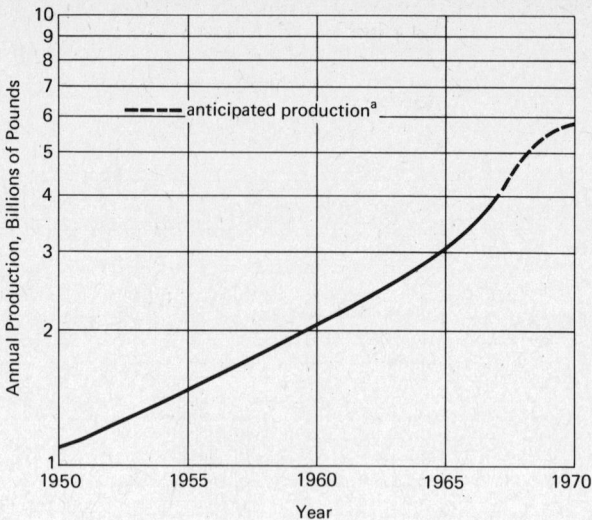

aTaking into account competition from other plastics such as polypropylene and poly-styrene.

Figure 14

A SEMILOGARITHMIC GRAPH, SHOWING
GROWTH IN POLYETHYLENE PRODUCTION IN THE
UNITED STATES, 1950-1968

Source: "Polyethylene—A New Commodity," *Chemical Purchasing* (May, 1967), Vol. 3, No. 4, pp. 17-18.

Area Diagrams. In an area diagram different quantities of a variable are represented by different spatial areas. They can be parts of a larger area, for example, wedges of a circle, or whole areas of varying sizes, for instance, a series of circles or rectangles.

The most widely used area diagram is the "pie graph." To remedy a major disadvantage of the area diagram—the impossibility of accurately esti-mating the relative sizes of the segments—each segment should be labeled with the correct percentage of the whole that it represents.

Placing Graphs in the Text

All graphs, illustrations, and the like must be referred to in the text of your manuscript. As with tables, the logical place is the first instance in which the material is to be used by the reader. Call attention to the figure by a few introductory words, such as one of the following:

Figure 1 shows that . . .
This is clearly shown in Figure 2 where . . .
A comparison of Figures 3 and 4 demonstrates . . .
See Figure 5 . . .

In both reference and placement the same rules apply as for tables (see Chapter 12, particularly "Table Placement" and "Discussion of the Table").

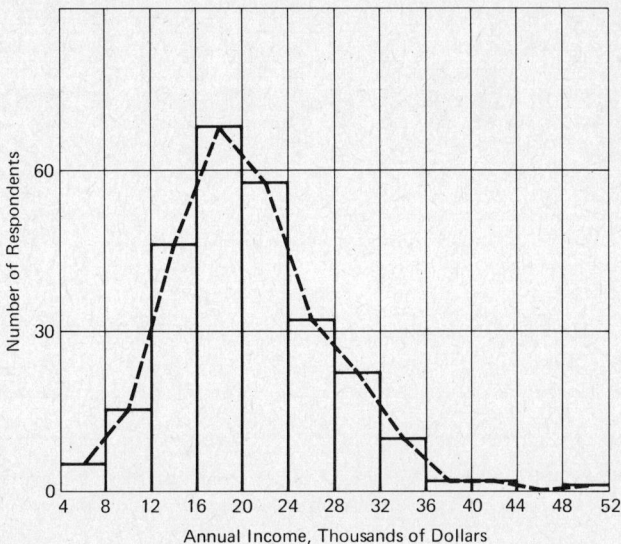

Figure 15

A HISTOGRAM, SHOWING THE DISTRIBUTION OF ANNUAL INCOME
AMONG RESPONDENTS TO THE MARKET STUDY, CORRECTED TO 1967 DOLLARS

Completeness and Numbering

Be careful that you do not use the figure to present information that is more appropriately included in an appendix, if at all. Make your illustration as simple as you can. To avoid internal crowding, abbreviations may be used if they can be readily understood by the reader.

Pages on which figures appear are numbered within the sequence of the text pages. Rules for margins, folding oversized illustrations, and so on can be found in Chapter 12. Each graph and illustration is also numbered with Arabic numerals preceded by the capitalized word "figure"; this label should be typed *below* the illustration or graph. Figures are numbered sequentially throughout the manuscript. See "Table Numbers," Chapter 12.

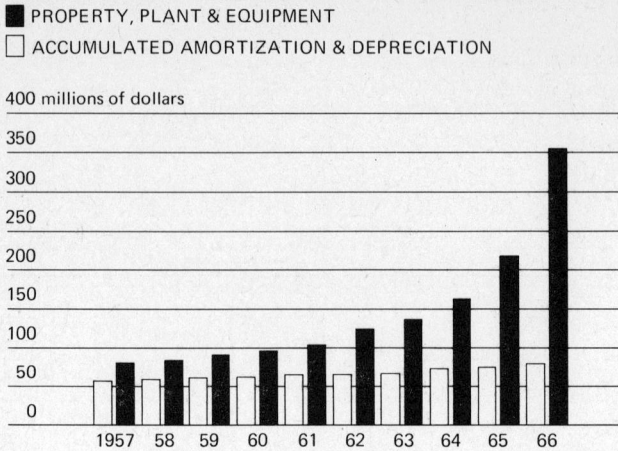

400 millions of dollars

350

300

250

200

150

100

50

0

1957 58 59 60 61 62 63 64 65 66

Figure 16

A SAMPLE BAR GRAPH ILLUSTRATING
SOME RESOURCES OF THE TEXAS GULF SULFUR COMPANY

Source: Reproduced with permission from *Annual Report, 1966* (New York: The Texas Gulf Sulfur Company, 1967), p. 4.

THE BUDGET DOLLAR

Where it comes from . . .

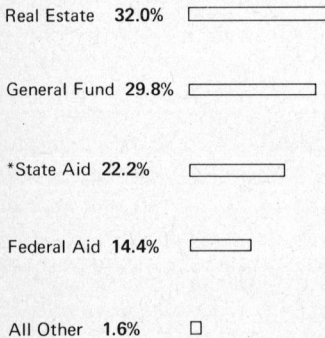

Real Estate **32.0%**

General Fund **29.8%**

*State Aid **22.2%**

Federal Aid **14.4%**

All Other **1.6%**

Includes state aid credited to the General Fund

What it is spent for . . .

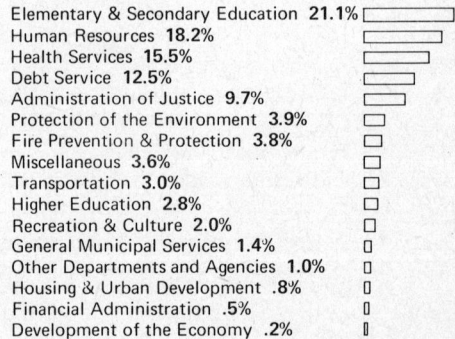

Elementary & Secondary Education **21.1%**
Human Resources **18.2%**
Health Services **15.5%**
Debt Service **12.5%**
Administration of Justice **9.7%**
Protection of the Environment **3.9%**
Fire Prevention & Protection **3.8%**
Miscellaneous **3.6%**
Transportation **3.0%**
Higher Education **2.8%**
Recreation & Culture **2.0%**
General Municipal Services **1.4%**
Other Departments and Agencies **1.0%**
Housing & Urban Development **.8%**
Financial Administration **.5%**
Development of the Economy **.2%**

Figure 17

A SUBDIVIDED PERCENTAGE BAR CHART
SHOWING THE SOURCE AND DISPOSITION OF THE MUNICIPAL BUDGET

Source: Reproduced with permission from *The New York Times* (August 22, 1965), Vol. 114, No. 39,292, p. 47, col. 3. © 1965 by *The New York Times* Company.

The Title

The same rules apply to figure legends as to table titles, with two exceptions: the title of a figure goes below the figure, and the inverted-pyramid design is optional for long titles. You may also type the lines flush left.

Figure Margins and Folding

The margin requirements for figures, as well as the rules for folding large graphs and illustrations, are the same as those for tables. See Chapter 12.

Drawing and Lettering

Graphs and illustrations should be drawn in black ink whenever they cannot be typed. This rule applies to both line work and lettering. It is far better to use different kinds of lines—solid, broken, and dotted, for example—than to use colored inks, for colors can seldom be differentiated when the figure is mechanically reproduced.

Footnotes and Source Notes

A footnote is used to amplify, qualify, or supplement data in a figure. A key, which is a type of footnote used to explain some aspect of the figure—for example, a mileage scale or the meaning of dotted and dashed lines—should be inserted *within* the confines of the figure itself if there is room and no confusion is likely to result.

If you yourself have compiled the data presented, you need not cite its source. Otherwise the same rules for citing sources apply for figures as for tables. The source note is placed after the figure legend.

Use of Materials

If you must submit photographs, printed forms, or other such material with your manuscript, mount them with rubber cement on the same kind of paper that you are using for the rest of your manuscript, whenever possible. Sometimes, however, special paper is necessary for certain figures. Graph paper preprinted with grids for arithmetic, semilogarithmic, logarithmic, and other scales is one example. Machine copies, photostats, blueprints, and so on are also acceptable. The rule to follow is to use the paper that permits the greatest clarity of illustration. Photostating, by the way, permits you to reduce or enlarge illustrations to suit your requirements.

Bibliography

Blickle, Margaret, and Kenneth Houp, *Reports for Science and Industry* (New York: Henry Holt and Co., 1958), pp. x + 320.

Comer, David, III, and Ralph Spillman, *Modern Technical and Industrial Reports* (New York: G. P. Putnam's Sons, 1962), pp. xix + 425.

Graves, Harold F., and Lyne Hoffman, *Report Writing* (4th ed.; Englewood Cliffs, New Jersey: Prentice-Hall, Inc., 1965), pp. viii + 286.

Hay, Robert, *Written Communications for Business Administrators* (New York: Holt, Rinehart and Winston, 1965), pp. xix + 487.

Sherman, Theodore, A., *Modern Technical Writing* (2nd ed.; Englewood Cliffs, New Jersey: Prentice-Hall, Inc., 1966), pp. xvii + 418.

Ulman, Joseph, Jr., and Jay Gould, *Technical Reporting* (New York: Henry Holt and Co., 1959), pp. vii + 382.

Winfrey, Robley, *Technical and Business Report Preparation* (3rd ed.; Ames, Iowa: Iowa State University Press, 1962), pp. x + 340.

chapter 14
style [1]

Every author has his own individual writing style. But the mechanics of punctuation, capitalization, word division, abbreviation, and grammar should follow accepted style. A general knowledge of this style will facilitate not only your writing but also the ease with which readers will understand your manuscript. Both scholars and business executives will have more respect for contents presented according to the highest standards.

Capitalization

Capitalize only when there is specific need or reason to do so. Many writers have a tendency to use capitals unnecessarily. When in doubt, one can usually learn whether a particular word is generally capitalized by consulting the dictionary.

Capitalize the first word of a sentence. Capitalize, also, any word (or the first word of a phrase) that stands independently as though it were a sentence.

> He is the new president of the corporation.
> Where is the organization chart?
> Hallelujah! Unemployment declined!

Capitalize the first word of a direct quotation within a sentence (unless the quotation is a fragment).

> He replied, "Knowledge is power."
> "Turner," he asked, "don't you want to join this conference?"
> He denied that he was "a major stockholder."

Capitalize all proper nouns and adjectives:

Italians
the Vanderbilt family
Australia
Chicago

[1] Pages 113–137 of this chapter have been adapted from *The Random House Dictionary of the English Language* (New York: Random House, Inc., 1966), pp. 1896-1901, by permission of Random House, Inc. ©Copyright 1969, 1967, 1966 by Random House, Inc.

Do not capitalize words derived from proper nouns but now having a special meaning distinct from the proper name:

pasteurize
china
macadam

Capitalize recognized geographical names:

Ohio River
Cascade Mountains
Strait of Juan de Fuca
Gulf of Mexico

Capitalize the following when they follow a single proper name and are written in the singular:

Butte
Canyon
County
Creek
Delta
Gap
Glacier
Harbor
Head
Ocean
Peninsula
Plateau
Range
River
Valley

For example, the *Sacramento River,* but the *Tennessee and Cumberland rivers.*

Capitalize the following in the singular and plural when they follow a proper name:

Hill
Island
Mountain
Narrows

Capitalize the following in the singular whether placed before or after the name. Capitalize in the plural when they come before the name and sometimes following a single name:

Bay
Point
Strait
Sea
Cape
Desert
Gulf
Isle
Lake
Mount
Peak
Plain

For example, *Lakes George and Champlain* but *Malheur and Goose lakes.*

Capitalize compass directions when they designate particular regions. Capitalize also the nicknames or special names for regions or districts:

East Tennessee
Middle Atlantic States
the New World
the South
the Near East
the Dust Bowl

Exception: Do not capitalize merely directional parts of states or countries.

eastern Washington
southern Indiana

Capitalize the names of streets, parks, buildings, etc.:

Fifth Avenue
Metropolitan Opera House
Central Park
Empire State Building

Exceptions: Do not capitalize such categories of buildings as *library, post office,* or *museum,* written without a proper name, unless local custom makes the classification equivalent to a proper name.

Capitalize the names of organizations, institutions, political parties, alliances, movements, classes, religious groups, nationalities, races, etc.:

Democratic party
Republicans

Protestants
United Nations
American Legion
Negroes
Axis powers
Soviet Russia
University of Wisconsin
Lutherans
Dutch Treat Club
Caucasians

Capitalize divisions, departments, and offices of government, when the official name is used. Do not capitalize incomplete or roundabout designations:

Department of Commerce
Circuit Court of Marion County
Bureau of Labor Statistics
Congress
Senate
United States Army
Board of Aldermen
the council
the lower house (of Congress)
the bureau
the legislature

Capitalize the names of wars, battles, treaties, documents, prizes, and important periods or events:

the Battle of the Bulge
Declaration of Independence
Nobel Prize
Revolutionary War
Congress of Vienna
Black Death
War of 1812
Golden Age of Pericles
Middle Ages
Treaty of Versailles

Do not capitalize *war* or *treaty* when used without the distinguishing name.

Capitalize the numerals used with kings, dynasties, or organizations. Numerals preceding the name are ordinarily spelled out; those following the name are commonly put in Roman numerals:

    Second World War
    Nineteenth Amendment
    Forty-eighth Congress
    World War II
    Third Army
    Henry IV

Capitalize titles, ranks of honor, military or civil, academic degrees, decorations, etc., when written with the name, and all titles of honor or rank when used for specific persons in place of the name:

    General Eisenhower
    the Senator from Ohio
    King George
    the Archbishop of Canterbury
    Mr. President

Capitalize the main words (nouns, verbs, adjectives, adverbs) of the titles of books, articles, poems, plays, musical compositions, etc., as well as the first word:

    A Treasury of the World's Great Speeches
    Rockets and Missiles
    House of Commons

Titles of chapters in a book are usually capitalized. Capitalize also any sections of a specific book, such as *Bibliography, Index, Table of Contents,* etc.

In expressions of time, A.M., P.M., A.D., and B.C. are usually written or typed in capitals without space between them.

    9:40 A.M.
    12 P.M.
    42 B.C.
    6:10 P.M.
    A.D. 1491

It is equally acceptable to show *a.m.* and *p.m.* in lower-case letters. When A.M., P.M., A.D., and B.C. are to be typeset, one may mark them with double-underlining to indicate that small capitals are to be used.

Italics

Italics (indicated by underlining in manuscript) are occasionally used to emphasize a particular word, phrase, or statement. Done with restraint, this use of italics can be effective. Done to excess, it reduces the text to a flickering mass.

Italics are used when referring to the titles of books, magazines, newspapers, motion pictures and plays, longer musical compositions, works of art, ships, aircraft, and book-length poems.

Business Periodicals Index
Magazine of Wall Street
The New York Times
Cost Accounting
Saturn Rocket

Foreign words and phrases that are used in English texts should always be italicized.

We closed the seminar to wish him *bon voyage.*
I'll be there, *deo volente.*

Use italics when referring to a letter, number, word, or expression as such. Quotation marks are sometimes used instead of italics.

The word *dynamic* is his favorite adjective.
He drew a large *4* on the blackboard to indicate a target.

Division of Words

The division of a word at the end of a line should be avoided. If it is necessary to divide a word, follow the syllabification shown in the dictionary.

Do not syllabify a word so that only one letter stands alone at the end or beginning of a line. Do not divide a one-syllable word, including words ending in *-ed* (such as *walked, saved, hurled*). Avoid the division of a word that carries only two letters over to the next line. The following terminal parts of words should never be divided: *-able, -ible; -cial, -sial, -tial; -cion, -sion, -tion; -gion; -ceous, -cious, -tious; -geous.*

If a word that already has a hyphen must be broken, hyphenate only at the hyphen.

	commander- in-chief	commander-in- chief
but not	command- er-in-chief	

Punctuation

Period (.). Use a period:
1. To end a declarative or imperative sentence (but not an exclamatory sentence).

The meeting was amicable and constructive.
Please pass the proxies.
Read the next two reports before Friday.

2. To end an indirect question.

Tell us when the plane is leaving.

3. To follow most abbreviations.

Ellipsis (. . . or . . . .). Use an ellipsis mark (three or four consecutive periods) to indicate that part of a quoted sentence has been omitted.

1. If the omission occurs at the beginning or in the middle of the sentence, use three periods in the ellipsis.

". . . the report is accurate . . . and well written."

2. If the last part of the sentence is omitted or if entire sentences are omitted, add a fourth period to the ellipsis to mark the end of the sentence.

"He left our firm . . . . Years later he returned as an executive to find that everything had changed. . . ."

Question Mark (?). Use a question mark:
1. To end a sentence, clause, or phrase (or after a single word) that asks a question.

Who placed him on the committee?
"Is something wrong?" he asked.
Who said "When?"
Whom shall we elect? Smith? Jones?

2. To indicate doubt or uncertainty.

The manuscript dates back to 1929(?).

Exclamation Point (!). Use an exclamation point to end a sentence, clause, or phrase (or after a single word) that indicates strong emotion or feeling, especially surprise, command, admiration, etc.

Cancel it!
What a day this has been!
"Raise the margin!" he ordered.
"Superior!"

Comma (,). Use a comma:
1. To separate words, phrases, and clauses that are part of a series of three or more items.

The Danes are an industrious, friendly, generous, and hospitable people. The chief agricultural products of Denmark are butter, eggs, potatoes, beets, wheat, barley, and oats.

It is permissible to omit the final comma before the *and* in a series of words as long as the absence of a comma does not interfere with clarity of meaning. The final commas in the examples above, while desirable, are not essential.

In many cases, however, the inclusion or omission of a comma before the conjunction can materially affect the meaning. In the following sentence, omission of the final comma might indicate that the tanks were amphibious.

Their equipment included airplanes, helicopters, artillery, amphibious vehicles, and tanks.

Do not use commas to separate two items treated as a single unit within a series.

The breakfast menu included orange juice, bread and butter, coffee, and bacon and eggs.

But

The cafeteria had to buy the following for the breakfast meeting: orange juice, bread, butter, bacon, and eggs.

2. Do not use commas to separate adjectives which are so closely related that they appear to form a single element with the noun they modify. Adjectives which refer to the number, age (*old, young, new*), size, color, or location of the noun often fall within this category. A simple test can usually determine the appropriateness of a comma in such instances: If *and* can not replace the comma without creating a clumsy, almost meaningless effect, it is safe to conclude that a comma is also out of place.

ten happy young clerks were promoted
a dozen large new mahogany desks

But commas must be used in the following cases where clarity demands separation of the items in a series.

a dozen large mahogany, walnut, and oak desks
twenty young, middle-aged, and old managers

In a series of phrases or dependent clauses, place a comma before the conjunction.

He sold his business, rented his house, gave up his car, paid his creditors, and set off for his new assignment in Denmark.
They strolled along the aisles, spot-checked the inventory, and verified the data.

3. To separate independent clauses joined by the coordinating conjunctions *and, but, yet, for, or, nor.*

Almost any man knows how to earn money, but not one in a million knows how to spend it.

The comma may be omitted in sentences consisting of two short independent clauses.

The salesmen missed the plane for Washington but they caught the train in time.

4. To separate a long introductory phrase or subordinate clause from the rest of the sentence.

Having rid themselves of their former officers, the stockholders now disagreed on the new leadership.
Scientists are confident of man's reaching the moon, although the details have not been fully developed.

5. To set off words of direct address, interjections, or transitional words used to introduce a sentence (*oh, yes, no, however, nevertheless, still, anyway, well, why, frankly, really, moreover, incidentally,* etc.).

Smith, where have you been?
Oh, here's our new statistician.
Why, you can't mean that!
Still, you must agree that he knows his business.
Fine, we'll get together.
Well, can you imagine that!

6. To set off an introductory modifier (adjective, adverb, participle, participial phrase) even if it consists of only one word or a short phrase.

As a diplomat, our chairman has proved to be inept.
Hurt, he left the room quickly.
Pleased with the result, he beamed at his bonus.

7. To set off a nonrestrictive clause or phrase (an element which is not essential to the basic meaning of the sentence). Place commas both before and after the nonrestrictive portion.

The reception hall, which had housed visiting celebrities for almost fifty years, remained outwardly unchanged.

8. To set off appositives or appositive phrases. Place commas both before and after the appositive.

March, the month of crocuses, can still bring snow and ice.
One of our major problems, synthetic leather, is solved.
Mr. Case, a member of the committee, refused to comment.

9. To set off parenthetical words and phrases and words of direct address.

You may, if you insist, demand a retraction.
The use of pesticides, however, has its disadvantages.
We knew, nevertheless, that the account was lost.
Mr. Brown, far younger in spirit than his sixty years, delighted in his new assignment.
You realize, Mr. Phelps, that we may close our plant here.

10. To set off quoted matter from the rest of the sentence. (See *Quotation Marks* below.)

11. To set off items in dates and titles of individuals.

Both John Adams and Thomas Jefferson died on July 4, 1826, just fifty years after the Declaration of Independence.

A comma may or may not be used when only two items are given in a date.

Washington was born in February, 1732, in Virginia.

or

Washington was born in February 1732, in Virginia.

12. To set off elements in addresses and geographical locations when the items are written on the same line.

35 Fifth Avenue, New York, N.Y.
1515 Halsted Street, Chicago, Illinois.
He sold shoes in Lima, Peru, for fifteen years.

13. To set off titles of individuals.

Dr. Martin Price, Dean of Admissions
Mr. John Winthrop, President

14. To set off the salutation in a personal letter.

Dear Fred,

15. To set off the closing in a letter.

Sincerely yours,
Very truly yours,

16. To denote an omitted word or words in one or more parallel constructions within a sentence.

John is studying Greek; George, French.

Semicolon (;). Use a semicolon:
1. To separate independent clauses not joined by a conjunction.

The account was lost; it was the last shattering blow.
The research must continue; we must be satisfied only with success.

2. To separate independent clauses that are joined by such conjunctive adverbs as *hence, however, therefore,* etc.

The funds are inadequate; therefore, the project will close down.
Enrollments exceed all expectations; however, there is a teacher shortage.

3. To separate long or possibly ambiguous items in a series, especially when the items already include commas.

> The elected officers are Jonathan Crane, president; Frances Glenn, vice president; Edward Morrell, treasurer; and Susan Stone, secretary.

4. To separate elements that are closely related but cannot be joined unambiguously.

> Poverty is unbearable; luxury, insufferable.

5. To precede an abbreviation or word that introduces an explanatory or summarizing statement.

> On the advice of his broker, after much deliberation, he chose to invest in major industries; i.e., steel, automobiles, and oil.
> He organized his work well; for example, by putting correspondence in folders of different colors to indicate degrees of urgency.

Colon (:). Use a colon:
1. To introduce a series or list of items, examples, or the like.

> The three committees are as follows: membership, finance, and nominations.

2. To introduce a long formal statement, quotation, or question.

> This I believe: All men are created equal and must enjoy equally the rights that are inalienably theirs.
> The President replied: "You are right. There can be no unilateral peace just as there can be no unilateral war. No one will contest that view."
> This is the issue: Can an employer dismiss a man simply because he laughs loudly?

Note that the first word of the sentence following the colon is capitalized.

3. To follow a formal salutation, as in a letter or speech.

> Dear Mr. Chadwin:
> My Fellow Americans:
> To Whom It May Concern:

4. To separate parts of a citation.

> Genesis 3:2.
> Journal of Astronomy 15:261-327.

5. To separate hours from minutes in indicating time.

> 1:30 P.M.

6. To indicate that an initial clause in a sentence will be further explained or illustrated by the material which follows the colon. In effect, the colon is a substitute for such phrases as "for example," or "namely."

Our factory was in a city notorious for its inadequacies: Its schools were antiquated, its administration was corrupt, and everyone felt the burden of its taxes.

Apostrophe ('). Use an apostrophe:
1. To denote the omission of letters, figures, or numerals.
a. The contraction of a word:

nat'l
ma'am
I'm
she's
m'f'g
couldn't
you're
we're
ne'er
won't
he's
they're

Do not confuse *it's* (contraction of *it is*) with the possessive *its*, which does not contain an apostrophe.
b. The contraction of a number, usually a date:

the Spirit of '76
the Sales Campaign of '68

c. The omission of letters in quoting dialect:

"I ain't goin' back 'cause I'm doin' mighty fine now."

2. To denote the possessive case of nouns.
a. To form the possessive of most singular and plural nouns or of indefinite pronouns not ending in *s*, add an apostrophe and an *s*.

the city's industries
the women's clubs
someone's car
bachelor's degree

b. To form the possessive of singular nouns (both common and proper) ending in *s* or the sound of *s*, add an apostrophe and an *s* in most instances.

the bus's signal light
John Holmes's reports
Kansas's schools
Texas's governor
the class's average
Francis's promotion

But if the addition of an *s* would produce an awkward or unpleasant sound or visual effect, add only an apostrophe.

Jones' concepts
for goodness' sake
for old times' sake

In some cases either form is acceptable.

Mr. Jones's or Jones' employees
Sears' or Sears's Television sets

c. To form the possessive of plural nouns (both common and proper) ending in *s*, add only an apostrophe.

manufacturers' problems
students' views
critics' reviews
two weeks' vacation
judges' opinions
the Smiths' travels
the Joneses' relatives
three months' delay

Note, however, that plurals not ending in *s* form their possessive by adding the apostrophe and *s*.

men's clothing
women's hats

d. To denote possession in most compound constructions, add the apostrophe and *s* to the last word of the compound.

anyone else's property
one another's books
supervisor's job
the attorney general's office

e. To denote joint possession by two or more proper names, add the apostrophe and *s* to the last name only.

Brown, Ross and King's law firm
United State and Germany's agreement

f. To denote individual ownership by two or more proper names, add the apostrophe and an *s* to both names.

Gimbel's and Macy's advertisements

3. To form the plurals of letters or figures add an apostrophe and an *s.*

Dot the i's and cross the t's.
33 r.p.m.'s
figure 8's
t's
+'s and –'s
the 1970's (or 1970s)
P.X.'s
C.O.'s
V.I.P.'s
G.I.'s

Quotation Marks (" "). Use quotation marks:
1. To distinguish spoken words from other matter, as in reporting dialogue.

"Knowledge is the foundation of good writing!" said Horace.

2. To mark single words, sentences, paragraphs, or poetic stanzas which are quoted verbatim from the original.

Portia's speech on "the quality of mercy" is one of the most quoted passages from Shakespeare.
It was Disraeli who wrote: "The best way to become acquainted with a subject is to write a book about it."

3. To enclose a quotation within a quotation, in which case a single quotation mark is used.

Reading Brown's letter, the manager said, "Listen to this! 'I've just received notice that I sold my quota.' Isn't that great?"

4. To enclose titles of newspaper and magazine articles, essays, stories, poems, and chapters of books. The quotation marks are designed to distinguish such literary pieces from the books or periodicals (these are italicized) in which they appear.

Our report contains citations from such widely assorted sources as Bacon's essay "Of Studies," Poe's "The Gold Bug," Keats's "Ode to a Nightingale," and an article on criticism from *The Saturday Review.*

5. To emphasize a word or phrase which is itself the subject of discussion.

> The words "imply" and "infer" are not synonymous.
> Such terms as the "coke," "drug store," and the "weekend" are now considered part of the French language.

6. To draw attention to an uncommon word or phrase, a technical term, or a usage very different in style (dialect, extreme slang) from the context. Italics are often used for the same purpose.

> Teachers need not be dismayed when students smirk at "square" traditions.
> In glassblowing, the molten glass is called "metal."

7. To suggest ironic use of a word or phrase.

> The TV blasting forth Jones's favorite "commercial" becomes an instrument of torture.
> Smith's skiing "vacation" consisted of three weeks with his leg in a cast.

The placement of quotation marks is determined by certain arbitrary rules and varies with different marks of punctuation.

1. Use quotation marks both before and after a quoted word, phrase, or longer passage.

2. Use a comma between the quoted matter and such phrases as "according to the speaker," "he said," "she replied," "they asked," whenever these phrases introduce a quotation, are used parenthetically, or follow a quotation which, in its original form, would end with a period.

> According to the by-laws, "each share of preferred stock has one vote."
> "Well," announced Mr. Frank, "we are going to raise our goal next year."
> Jones asked, "Why not this year?"

3. Whenever such phrases as "he said," "he replied," or "he asked" follow a question or an exclamation, use the corresponding punctuation before the end quotation mark.

> "Why can't we ship this week?" asked MacMullen.
> "We simply can't. And that's final!" replied the manager.

4. Always place the end quotation mark *before* a colon or semicolon.

> He remembered that the men had always called Rusk "the champ"; he began to wonder if the reputation endured.
> There were several reasons why Rusk was acknowledged as "the champ": sales ability, intellectual superiority, and qualities of leadership.

5. Place the end quotation mark *after* a question mark or exclamation point only when the question or exclamation is part of the quoted passage.

"Expedite, please, before it's too late!" the salesman wrote.
"Is there any hope of recovering the property?" he asked.

In all other cases, place the quotation mark *before* the exclamation point or question mark.

Did Fulton really mean it when he said, "This is the best of all possible deals"?
How absurd of him to say "This is the best of all possible deals"!

6. If a quotation consists of two or more consecutive paragraphs, use quotation marks at the beginning of each paragraph, but place them at the end of the last paragraph only.

Parentheses ( ). Use parentheses:
1. To enclose material that is not part of the main sentence but is too relevant to omit.

Faulkner's novels (published by Random House) were selected as prizes.
Mr. Johnson (to the chairman): Will you allow that question to pass unanswered?
The data (see Table 13) was very impressive.

2. To enclose part of a sentence that, if enclosed by commas, would be confusing.

The authors he advised (none other than Hemingway, Lewis, and Cather) would have been delighted to honor him today.

3. To enclose an explanatory item that is not part of the statement or sentence.

He shipped the order to the Springfield (Ohio) depot.

4. To enclose numbers or letters that designate each item in a series.

The project is (1) too expensive, (2) too time-consuming, and (3) poorly staffed.
He was required to take courses in (a) accounting, (b) management, (c) marketing, and (d) finance.

5. To enclose a numerical figure used to confirm a spelled-out number which precedes it.

Enclosed is a check for ten dollars ($10.00) to cover the cost of the order.

Brackets [ ]. Brackets are used in pairs to enclose figures, phrases, or sentences that are meant to be set apart from the context—usually a direct quotation.
Use brackets:

1. To set off a notation, explanation, or editorial comment that is inserted in quoted material and is not part of the original text.

According to our best customer, "This [blue plastic container] is one of Shaw's finest products."

Or substitute the bracketed proper name for the pronoun: "[blue plastic container] is one of Shaw's. . . ."

"As a result of the Gemini V mission [the flight by astronauts Cooper and Conrad in August 1965], we have proof that man can withstand the eight days in space required for a round trip to the moon."
"Young as they are," he writes, "these students are afflicted with cynicism, world-weariness, and *a total disregard for tradition and authority*." [Emphasis is mine.]

2. To correct an error in a quotation.

"It was on April 25, 1944 [1945—Ed.] that delegates representing forty-six countries met in San Francisco."

3. To indicate that an error in fact, spelling, punctuation, or language usage is quoted deliberately in an effort to reproduce the original statement with complete accuracy. The questionable fact or expression is followed by the Latin word *sic*, meaning "thus," which is enclosed in brackets.

"George Washington lived during the seventeenth [sic] century."
"The governor of Missisipi [sic] addressed the student body."

4. To enclose comments made on a verbatim transcription of a speech, debate, or testimony.

Sen. Eaton: The steady rise in taxes must be halted. [Applause]

5. To substitute for parentheses within material already enclosed by parentheses. Although it is not seen frequently, this device is sometimes used in footnotes.

[1] See "Budgeting" (John G. Blocker and W. Keith Weltmer, *Cost Accounting* [New York: McGraw-Hill Book Co., Inc., 1954]).

6. To enclose the publication date, inserted by the editor, of an item appearing in an earlier issue of a periodical. This device is used in letters to the editor or in articles written on subjects previously reported. Parentheses may also be used for this purpose.

Dear Sir: Your excellent article on foreign-trade barriers [April 15] brings to mind my recent experience . . .
When removing old wallpaper [Homeowners' Monthly, March 1965] some do-it-yourselfers neglect to . . .

Brackets may be inserted by hand if your typewriter does not have them.

Dash (—). Use a dash:

1. To mark an abrupt change in thought or grammatical construction in the middle of a sentence.

> Our competitor gained our client—but I'm getting ahead of the story.

2. To suggest halting or hesitant speech.

> "Well—er—ah—it's hard to explain," he faltered.

3. To indicate a sudden break or interruption before a sentence is completed.

> "Johnson, don't sell that—." It was too late.

4. To add emphasis to parenthetical material or to mark an emphatic separation between parenthetical material and the rest of a sentence.

> His influence—he was a powerful figure in the trade—was a deterrent to effective opposition.
> The excursions for school groups—to museums, zoos and theatres—are less expensive.
> The car he was driving—a gleaming red convertible—was the most impressive thing about him.

5. To set off an appositive or an appositive phrase when a comma would provide less than the desired emphasis on the appositive or when the use of commas might result in confusion with commas within the appositive phrase.

> The premier's promise of changes—land reform, higher wages, reorganization of industry—was not easily fulfilled.

Hyphen (-). The hyphenation of compound nouns and modifiers is often arbitrary, inconsistent, and subject to change. Practices vary. To determine current usage as well as traditional forms, it is best to consult the dictionary.

Use a hyphen:

1. To spell out a word or name.

> r-e-a-s-o-n
> T-e-x-a-c-o

2. To divide a word into syllables.

> hal-lu-ci-na-tion

3. To mark the division of a word of more than one syllable at the end of a line, indicating that the word is to be completed on the following line.

> It is difficult to estimate the damaging psychological effects of auto-mating the plant.

4. To separate the parts (when spelling out numerals) of a compound number from twenty-one to ninety-nine.

thirty-six inches to the yard
Fifty-second Street
nineteen hundred and sixty-eight

5. To express decades in words.

the nineteen-seventies
the eighteen-sixties

6. To separate (when spelling out numerals) the numerator from the denominator of a fraction, especially a fraction which is used as an adjective.

One-half gallon of gasoline
a two-thirds majority

While some authorities avoid hyphenating fractions used as nouns, the practice is not uncommon.

Three fourths (or three-fourths) of his employees
One fifth (or one-fifth) of the credit department

Do not use a hyphen to indicate a fraction if either the numerator or denominator is already hyphenated.

one thirty-second
forty-five hundredths
twenty-one thirty-sixths

7. To form certain compound nouns
a. Nouns consisting of two or more words which show the combination of two or more constituents, qualities, or functions in one person or thing.

secretary-treasurer
teacher-counselor
city-state
AFL-CIO

b. Nouns made up of two or more words, including other parts of speech.

cease-fire
short-sale
court-martial
cure-all
editor-in-chief
fourth-grader
has-been

jack-in-the-pulpit
post-mortem
teen-age market

Do not hyphenate compound nouns denoting chemical terms, military rank, or certain governmental positions.

hydrogen sulfide
sodium chloride
carbon tetrachloride
vice admiral
lieutenant governor
justice of the peace
sergeant at arms
brigadier general
lieutenant junior grade
attorney general

8. To connect the elements of a compound modifier when used *before* the noun it modifies. In most cases, the same modifier is not hyphenated if it *follows* the noun it modifies.

They engaged in hand-to-hand combat.
They fought hand to hand.

They endured a hand-to-mouth existence.
They lived hand to mouth.

a well-known expert
an expert who is well known

Do not hyphenate a compound modifier which includes an adverb ending in *ly* even when it is used before the noun.

the buyer's loose-fitting jacket
the buyer's loosely fitting jacket

the firm's well-guarded secret
the firm's carefully guarded secret

9. To distinguish a less common pronunciation or meaning of a word from its more customary usage.

a recreation hall	re-creation of a scene
to recover from an illness	re-cover the couch
to reform a sinner	re-form their lines

10. To prevent possible confusion in pronunciation if a prefix results in the doubling of a letter, especially a vowel.

anti-inflationary
co-ordinate
pre-eminent
re-election
co-op
pre-empt
re-enact
re-entry

The dieresis (¨) is sometimes, but less frequently, used over *e* and *o* to accomplish the same result:

coöp
reëntry

11. To join the following prefixes with *proper* nouns or adjectives.

anti	anti-American, anti-British
mid	mid-Victorian, mid-Atlantic, mid-August
neo	neo-Nazi, neo-Darwinism
non	non-European, non-Asian, non-Christian
pan	Pan-American, Pan-Slavic, Pan-African
pro	pro-French, pro-American
un	un-American, un-British

With few exceptions, these prefixes are joined to common nouns without hyphenation:

anticlimax
nonintervention
midsummer
neoclassic
proslavery
unambiguous

12. To join the following prefixes and suffixes with the main word of a compound.

co-	co-chairman, co-worker, co-author
ex-	ex-sergeant, ex-mayor, ex-premier, ex-manager
self-	self-preservation, self-defeating, self-explanatory, self-educated
-elect	president-elect, director-elect

Abbreviations

In standard business, academic, scientific, or other organizational reports and correspondence, abbreviations are generally avoided unless they are the commonly required ones and are specifically known and accepted terms within a particular discipline or trade.

Some abbreviations that are acceptable in business or journalisitc writing may not be appropriate in extremely formal announcements or invitations in which even dates are spelled out.

Abbreviations are often used in ordering and billing, catalogues, tabulations, telephone books, classified advertising and similar cases where brevity is essential.

In some cases, the decision to use an abbreviation is a matter of individual preference. When in doubt, it is usually prudent to use the spelled-out form. Do not, however, spell out a word in one sentence or paragraph only to use the abbreviated form elsewhere. As in all writing, it is most important to maintain consistency of usage within any single written document, whether it be a letter or a treatise.

Use abbreviations in writing:

1. The following titles and forms of address whenever they precede a proper name: Mr., Mrs., Dr., Mme., Mlle., M. Do not spell out these titles even in the most formal situations.

> Mlle. Modiste
> Mr. Carl Sandburg
> Dr. Kildare
> Mme. Curie

2. Except in an extremely formal context, titles of the clergy, government officials, officers of organizations, military and naval personnel, provided that the title is followed by a first name or initial as well as a surname. If the title is followed only by a surname, it must be spelled out.

Gen. Dwight D. Eisenhower	General Eisenhower
Sgt. Leon Greene	Sergeant Greene
Prof. Richard L. Page	Professor Page
Gov. Nelson Rockefeller	Governor Rockefeller
Rev. John McDermott	The Reverend John Mc Dermott *or*
	The Reverend Dr. (*or* Mr.) McDermott
Hon. Eugene McCarthy	The Honorable Eugene McCarthy *or*
	The Honorable Mr. McCarthy

Note above that in very formal writing, the titles *Honorable* and *Reverend* are spelled out and are preceded by *The.* When the first name or initial is omitted, the title Mr. or Dr. is substituted.

3. *Jr.* or *Sr.* following a name. These abbreviations should be added only when the names preceding them include a first name or initial.

4. *Esq.* following a name. Not a common usage in the United States, this abbreviation should not be used with any other title.

James Grant, Esq. *not* Mr. James Grant, Esq.

5. Academic degrees: B.A. (Bachelor of Arts); M.A. (Master of Arts); M.S. (Master of Science); Ph.D. (Doctor of Philosophy); M.D. (Doctor of Medicine), etc. When a name is followed by a scholastic degree or by the abbreviations of religious or fraternal orders (BPOE) it should not be preceded by *Mr., Miss, Dr.,* or any other title.

6. The terms used to describe business firms (*Co., Corp., Inc., Bro.,* or *Bros., Ltd., R.R.* or *Ry.*) only when these abbreviations are part of the legally authorized name. In all other cases (except for brevity in tables, etc.), *Company, Corporation, Incorporated, Brothers,* and *Limited* should be spelled out.

7. Except in formal writing, the names of states, territories, or possessions that immediately follow the name of a city, mountain, airport, or other identifiable geographic locations. Check the dictionary for all such abbreviations.

Detroit, Mich.
San Juan, P.R.

8. Certain foreign expressions:

i.e. (*id est*), that is
e.g. (*exempli gratia*), for example
et al. (*et alii*), and others
etc. (*et cetera*), and so forth

Do not abbreviate:

1. Names of countries, except:
a. The U.S.S.R. (Union of Soviet Socialist Republics) because of its exceptional length.
b. U.S. (United States) when preceding the name of an American ship. The abbreviation U.S. may also be used in tables, footnotes, etc., when modifying a Government agency: U.S. Congress, U.S. Post Office, etc.

2. The words *street, avenue, boulevard, drive, square, road,* and *court,* except in lists requiring brevity.

3. The days of the week and the months of the year except in the most informal situations or in tables.

4. Weights and measures except in lists of items, technical writing, etc.

The firm had hoped to gain ten customers.
We used ten yards of cloth.

Do not use a period after the following abbreviations or shortened forms:

1. After a contraction, which is not to be confused with an abbreviation. Contractions contain apostrophes which indicate omitted letters; they never end with a period.

sec't'y or sec'y   sec.
Nat'l   natl.

2. After chemical symbols.

H_2O
$NaCl$

3. After *per cent*.

4. After initials of military services and specific military terms.

USA   United States Army
USAF   United States Air Force
USMC   United States Marine Corps
USN   United States Navy
USNR   United States Naval Reserve
USCG   United States Coast Guard
USNG   United States National Guard
MP   military police
SP   shore patrol
POW   prisoner of war
PX   post exchange
GI   government issue
APO   Army post office

5. After the initials of certain governmental agencies or call letters of television and radio stations.

NATO
SEATO
UNICEF
CIA
CARE
OES

CAP
WQXR
WINS

6. After letters that are used as symbols rather than initials.

Let us assume that A and B are playing opposite C and D.

7. After listed items (as in catalogues, outlines, or syllabi), if none of the items is a complete sentence. If the list includes only one complete sentence, use a period after this and all other items on the list, including those which are not complete sentences. Consistency is essential: a period after each item or no end punctuation whatever.

8. Points of the compass.

NE
ESE
SW
E by NE

Numbers

Numbers will appear throughout your manuscript; therefore it is best that you adhere to accepted rules for using them. Use Arabic numerals for numbers with three or more digits (124, not cxxiv). Write out all numbers requiring fewer than three digits (seventy-one, not 71); use numerals for numbers of one or two digits only to help clarify your text, for example, "seven 6-month sales trainees." Otherwise, numbers that can be expressed in one or two words should be: "Four rockets were launched last month; NASA plans to build eight next month." If a series of measurements contains some numerals of one or two digits and some of three digits or more (or when you are dealing with really mathematical material, as in statistical analysis), use numerals for *all* the numbers: "There were 17 office managers from the New England district, 24 from the Middle Atlantic region, and a total of 127 from all the other company sales districts attending the convention."

Try to avoid beginning a sentence with a number; rewrite the sentence or paragraph, if necessary. If you must begin with a number, then always spell it out: "Four hundred eighty-six applicants for employment were screened." There is no exception to this rule.

Spell out such simple fractions as one-half and one-hundredth. More complex fractions should be expressed decimally. Extremely small fractions can best be indicated by negative exponents, as in 8.2×10^{-5}. Fractions are customarily used for weights and measurements: 1/2-inch pipe.

Always use numerals for percentages. Remember that either "percent" or "per cent" is acceptable but that the percentage sign (%) should not be used in text: "89 percent" or "89 per cent."

Numerals are always acceptable in the following usages: as units of measurement (6 pounds, 5 feet, 4 inches, 72 miles, and so on); as decimals (10.74260); in any reference to numbered material ("The market share was shown repeatedly in Chapter 4; on pages 2, 13, 18, and 42; in Appendix E; and in equation 17"); in dates (October 12, 1492), addresses (136 Peachtree Drive), telephone numbers (949-6376), and times (1:45 P.M.); in sums of money, with appropriate symbols ($74.35, £5, 86 cents; if the sums are in round figures, as in $4, omit the decimal point and two zeros, unless other sums in the series or table require them).

Use commas in all numbers with four digits or more to the left of the decimal point, as in 1,054,672. Decimal numbers less than 1.0 should always be preceded by a zero: 0.523. Ordinal numbers (numbers that indicate ranking or serial position) are usually spelled out, with hyphens when necessary, as in these examples: "The first grade," "the Eighty-Second Congress," "Fifth Avenue," "the three hundred sixty-fifth day of the year."

When you must present more than two series of numbers in the same passage, present them in tabular form for clarity (see Chapter 12).

Lower-case Roman numerals (i, ii, iii, iv) are used mainly to indicate front-matter pages in books; capital Roman numerals are frequently used for volume numbers, numbers of the main parts in a book, or names, as in Louis XIV. Some publications print Roman numerals in small capitals.

Bibliography

Dugdale, Kathleen, *A Manual on Writing Research* (Bloomington, Indiana: Indiana University Bookstore, 1962), p. 50.

Hook, Julius N., *Guide to Good Writing: Grammar, Style, Usage* (New York: Ronald Press Co., 1962), pp. ix+ 515.

Gorrell, Robert M., and Charles Laird, *Modern English Handbook* (3rd ed.; Englewood Cliffs, New Jersey: Prentice-Hall, Inc., 1962), pp. xxiv + 645.

Lambuth, David, *The Golden Book on Writing* (New York: Viking Press, 1963), pp. xiv + 81.

Nelson, J. Raleigh, *Writing the Technical Report* (New York: McGraw-Hill Book Co., Inc., 1947), pp. xiv + 388.

Richards, Irving, and Paul Richards, *Proper Words in Proper Places* (Boston: Christopher Publishing House, 1964), p. 206.

Strunk, William, Jr., and E. B. White, *The Elements of Style* (New York: The Macmillan Co., 1959), pp. xiv + 71.

Wendell, Barrett, *English Composition* (New York: Frederick Ungar Publishing Co., 1963), pp. x + 316.

Woolley, Edwin, Franklin Scott, and Frederick Bracher, *College Handbook of English Composition* (Boston: D. C. Heath and Co., 1958), pp. xvi + 474.

Zetler, Robert, and W. G. Crouch, *Successful Communication in Science and Industry* (New York: McGraw-Hill Book Co., Inc., 1961), pp. vi + 290.

chapter 15
typing the manuscript

Eventually, the manuscript must be typed. A neat, well-done typescript presents the paper's content in its best light. No matter how objective the reader is, no matter how hard he tries to consider *only* the content, his judgment is substantially affected by the appearance of the text.

Aside from capitalizing upon the psychological connotations of the "package," many colleges and universities require specific typing formats. When no "official" prescriptions exist, there is usually at least a set of rules dictated by custom and utility. This chapter outlines standard typing requirements acceptable at most universities and other educational institutions.

Paper

The dissertation or thesis must last a long time and often receives extensive handling; the original copy should therefore be typed on sixteen- or twenty-pound bond paper, with a rag content of at least 25 percent, the grade of paper used by most business firms for correspondence. The size must be 8 1/2 × 11 inches and the color white. No deviation from these requirements is acceptable. As many schools now microfilm theses and dissertations, the paper's surface should be smooth; cockle and other textured surfaces do not lend themselves to photography. Be careful when using erasable paper; it has a tendency to smudge unless the ink has dried thoroughly. Many institutions forbid its use.

The student is ordinarily required to submit at least two copies of his manuscript. In addition, he must keep one for himself. Carbon copies are therefore necessary. They should be typed on a thin paper known as "onionskin."[1] Again white is the mandatory color. *Only one side of the paper is used.*

A good grade of carbon paper is essential for good copies. A black, medium-weight, hard-finished type is best. Change the carbon paper about every fifth page to ensure crisp, clear impressions. When several copies are to be made simultaneously, a light-weight, rather than a medium-weight, carbon paper should be tested for use—it may produce clearer impressions.

The development of electrostatic duplication processes, and improvements in multilithing and mimeographing, when coupled with the increased use

---

[1] Some schools require both the original and the duplicates to be typed on bond paper.

of electric typewriters, now makes carbon copies unnecessary in an increasing number of schools. Schools accept such reproductions, but will not generally approve a ditto copy.

Typewriter

Several factors are important in selecting the proper typewriter. The type should be pica, the standard size that gives ten characters or spaces to the inch. Many typewriters, particularly portable ones, have elite type, which gives twelve characters to the inch. Most institutions require pica type, except for large tables. There are a number of acceptable type faces; generally type should be plain and unobtrusive. Italics, script, Gothic, and other unusual faces are not acceptable.

The typewriter should be in good condition, its keys aligned and not deformed in any way. It is a relatively simple matter to have a machine with defects repaired. The keys must also be clean. Far too many students do not take the trouble to clean the keys of their typewriters. Any number of liquids and other substances are commercially available to do the job.

A variety of typewriter ribbons is available; a medium-inked black ribbon is the one to choose. Heavily inked ribbons smudge, and light ribbons are not dark enough to be read or microfilmed clearly and easily. Heavily inked ribbons also tend to lose their intensity rapidly, with the result that a manuscript that starts out with black type on the first page can fade to gray type by the twenty-fifth page. Even with the best medium-inked ribbons, there will be some fading as the typing progresses, but as long as it is not excessive the manuscript will be acceptable. To check, compare pages that are at least ten sheets apart. Do not discard the used ribbons; it is vital to have an assortment of such ribbons, of varying intensity, so that corrections made a week or even a month after the manuscript has been typed can be made to blend perfectly with the other words on the page and with the adjacent pages.

Special Symbols

Various mathematical and other symbols may be required, particularly by students in the sciences and engineering. Greek letters (Σ, Δ), chemical symbols ($\rightarrow, \rightleftharpoons$), symbols of foreign currencies (£), and the like can be handled in two ways. The first is to type them on a specially equipped machine (or to have a standard typewriter modified). This expensive approach is, however, seldom necessary. The easier method is simply to leave sufficient space for such special symbols and then to write them in carefully in black ink. They can be written freehand or with the aid of plastic or metal tracing forms available for this purpose.

Corrections

The guiding principle in making corrections is to present the reader with the best-looking manuscript possible. Some readers will insist upon near perfection, and you must therefore correct every mistake. If there are more than four mistakes on a page, it is usually easier and less time-consuming to retype the entire page.

Many aids are available for correction, but it is still an art that requires practice and patience. There must be *no* "strike-overs," crossed-out words or letters, or interlineations; this rule is absolute. When a letter or word needs changing, insert a 3 × 5-inch file card behind the master copy, and use one of the erasers manufactured specifically for typewriters. The file card will prevent the carbon copies from being smudged. So that *only* the mistake is erased, use a plastic or metal erasing shield. After erasing, it is often necessary to apply a light chalk coating to blot out the last traces of ink. Then lightly type the correct letter or word, and check to be sure that the intensity of the inking matches the adjacent words. If necessary, type the letter or word again.

Several manufacturers sell special correcting paper, which can be inserted under the ribbon and over the mistake; retyping the error transfers white chalk to the paper, which hides the error. Skill in the use of correcting papers is useful. Be certain, however, that the reproduction process you select (Xerox, 3M, or the like) does not pick up the errors; this caution is more important for theses and dissertations than for research papers, which usually need not be reproduced perfectly.

Each carbon copy must also be corrected, but it can usually be easily erased. The important point is to avoid smudging. Once carbon copies have been removed from the machine, each should be corrected separately. It is too difficult to realign the pages properly once they have been separated.

It is wise to review the typed page before removing it from the machine, for it is difficult to reinsert it in perfect alignment once it has been removed. When a page has to be retyped, be sure to use a ribbon of the proper intensity and to space the material so that the last line is of full length and the first line on the next page follows approximately.

Margins

Customary margin requirements are 1 1/2 inches at the left and top, 1 1/4 inches at the bottom, and 1 inch at the right. The bottom margin requirement must be adhered to even if it means that only one line will be typed on the next page. When illustrations or large tables must be included, margin requirements can sometimes be waived (see Chapter 12), but sufficient room must always be allowed at the left-hand margin for binding. For the first page of a chapter, bibliography, index, preface, or the like, a 1 1/2-inch top margin is required, though the other margins are the same.

All lines should be typed out to the right-hand margin; if words must be broken, do so according to syllables. Too many hypens at the right-hand margin look awkward, however, and you should try hard to avoid them. If necessary leave a gap at the end of a line. Avoid breaking words between two pages.

Indentations and Line Spacing

Various parts of the manuscript are indented from the left-hand margin. The first line of a paragraph is always indented five spaces (1/2 inch in pica type); every line of an extracted quotation is indented 1/2 inch from the left-hand margin.

The entire manuscript must be double-spaced. The exceptions are quotations (see Chapter 11), notes (see Chapter 10), bibliography (the spacing is the same as for notes), headings (four line spaces between the chapter title and the first line of text, three line spaces between the end line of a paragraph and an ensuing subheading, and three line spaces after a freestanding heading), and tables (see Chapter 12). The base lines of superscripts are typed about one-half of a space above the base line of the word to which they refer. Newer typewriters have half-spacing gears; older machines require that the platen be rotated.

Pagination

All pages should be numbered. All front matter (preceding the first page of Chapter 1) should be numbered with lower-case Roman numerals (i, ii, iii, iv). The title page is page i, but the number is not shown. The remaining pages (preface, table of contents, and so on) are numbered in the upper right-hand corner of the page, 1/2 inch below the top edge of the page and flush with the right-hand margin. See the numbering in the front of this book.

Beginning with the first page of Chapter 1, *every* page is numbered with an Arabic numeral. This statement applies to appendixes, bibliography, tables, figures, and so on. The number is placed just as in front matter. No periods are placed after page numbers and no hyphens before and after them.

When you find that you must insert an illustration or additional text after all the pages have been numbered, use the same number as that on the page preceding it, but add a lower-case letter: a, b, c, and so on.

Remember that every new part of the manuscript (chapter, bibliography, appendix, and so on) must begin on a new page. If a table runs to more than one page, each page must be given a separate number.

Typing Gauges

It is essential that the typist know precisely how far he is from the bottom and left-hand margins at any given moment. All typewriters have horizontal scales so that the typist can space from left to right with precision. The major problem is determining how much space remains above the bottom margin, so that footnotes can be fitted accurately into the page.

A few new-model typewriters have vertical guides, but most do not. The typist must use a guide sheet, which is inserted behind the first page of bond paper; this sheet is calibrated vertically from zero at the top down to the bottom edge. These numbers should show through the bond paper, revealing the exact position to the typist. Another kind of gauge sheet is wider than 8 1/2 inches, so that a numbered edge protrudes.

Typing Drafts

It is extremely difficult to type a first-rate final copy without a very good typed draft to work from. Each draft of your work should therefore conform as closely as possible to all the standards for the final version. Unless you begin by typing footnotes in the proper form, inserting page numbers in the appropriate position, constructing tables with the right spacing, indenting properly, and so on, errors are likely to be perpetuated. You can strike over words, interlineate phrases, and make marginal notations in a draft, but you should adhere as much as possible to format, style, and typing standards.

Proofreading

The manuscript must be carefully proofread not once but several times. Proofread each page before removing it from the typewriter, for corrections can most easily be made at that time. If they are minor erasing will suffice; if not the page should be retyped. The special advantages of proofreading are that realignment is usually unnecessary, that the intensity of carbon paper and ribbon are at hand and will be uniform, and that the flow of work will not be seriously interrupted. Serious mistakes caught at this point preclude the necessity for squeezing in extra lines, paragraphs, or pages or stretching out material to fill a page.

The second proofreading should follow completion of each major section of the work—chapter, appendix, or bibliography. After correction, the manuscript should then be put away for a week or two. This hiatus permits rereading with a fresh eye and with a mind which *reads* rather than remembers the material. Many errors can be caught this way; to be absolutely certain that no errors remain, ask someone else to proofread the paper too.

Actually, to be certain of a first-rate typescript, it is best to have the final draft typed by a professional, or at least an experienced typist who has enough time to do the job properly.

The standards for a term paper or report are seldom as exacting as those for a thesis or dissertation, but its appearance will be enhanced immeasurably by conformity with the standards set for graduate treatises.

Techniques for Emphasis

Skillful writers use various techniques to emphasize key points, words, phrases, and the like in their manuscripts. Primarily, of course, emphasis should be conveyed through organization and language, but some typographical devices are also useful.

The most common technique is judicious underscoring of headings and important words, phrases, even sentences. Too much underscoring dilutes its impact, however. Terms of outstanding importance can also be capitalized, even with extra spacing between letters.

Some symbols also help to highlight parts of the text. Careful use of exclamation points, asterisks, parentheses, quotation marks, commas, colons, brackets, dashes, ellipses, and the like can add significantly to the total impact of your work by directing the reader's attention so that he can better appreciate your line of thought.

Quotations, carefully selected, also can serve to alert the reader to points worthy of emphasis. Test your reaction to the quotation from Peter F. Drucker in Chapter 11.

Colored type or ink makes data, words, phrases, names or sentences stand out. Underscoring in color is also effective. Graphs, tables, or illustrations especially can be clarified with color. Remember, however, that color differences will not reproduce either photographically or on carbon copies.

Headings and subheadings are very important devices for clarifying the organizational emphasis in your work (see Chapter 9). The mere addition of graphs, tables, illustrations, photographs, advertisements, samples, and the like throughout the purely expository pages of a manuscript tends to intensify the reader's interest and make the work more meaningful to him.

Figure 18 is an example of how thesis pages can be presented.

Chapter 3

THE PRODUCT ABANDONMENT MODEL

It is the purpose of the product abandonment model to integrate the various perspectives of product elimination strategies. This integration combines, in compatible terms, evaluations of the quantitative and qualitative, of the tangible and intangible factors which bear upon the abandonment decision. The result, which this chapter presents, is a model that structures these factors into a cohesive and unified frame that is operationally effective in marketing decision-making.

THE GENERAL MODEL

Fortunately, some work has been done in the last decade in formulating systems of operations analysis which contribute to the construction of the necessary model.[1] The general form of such a system, termed the "Method of Weighting

---

[1] Frank M. Bass et al., Mathematical Models and Methods in Marketing (Homewood, Illinois: Richard D. Irwin, Inc., 1961), pp. 35-37, 42, passim.

Figure 18

A SAMPLE CHAPTER PAGE

Figure 18 (Cont'd.)

Objectives," and incorporated as an element of a product abandonment model, is described below.

The Method of Weighting Objectives

What the method does is to establish a system for estimating the relative value of a set of objectives or events. It weights the outcome of these activities in common terms, side-stepping many of the problems that usually arise in attempting to compare intangible with quantitative valuations. The procedure consists, broadly speaking, of a systematic check upon relative judgments by a process of successive comparisons.

Elements of the Model

The way these carefully weighed judgments can be applied to product elimination decisions has been presented by Berenson in a previous paper.[2] In that paper, it was shown that decision models for product pruning situations must contain some rather specific elements.

These elements may be grouped, for convenience in analysis and ease of understanding, into five categories. These categories are discussed below.

Group 1. The first group of factors to be considered may be subsumed under the heading of "Financial Security." Financial security refers to the basic profit criteria of the firm which are applied to the existing product and resources. This is frequently expressed in terms of a return on investment.[3]

---

[2] Conrad Berenson, "Pruning the Product Line", Business Horizons (Summer, 1963), Vol. 6, No. 2, pp. 63-70.

[3] Henry Jones, "Return on Investment as a Decision Criterion", Journal of Marketing (July, 1967), Vol. 31, No. 3, pp. 72-73, 76.

Bibliography

Altholz, Nathaniel, and Gertrude Altholz, *Modern Typewriter Practice* (2nd ed.; New York: Pitman Publishing Corp., 1957), pp. viii + 352.

Babcock, C. Merton, *The Harper Handbook of Communication Skills* (New York: Harper & Brothers, 1957), pp. xiv + 489.

Grossman, Jack, and Sherwood Friedman, *Handbook for Typists* (New York: Pitman Publishing Co., 1957) p. 72.

Lessenberry, D. D., S. J. Wanous, and C. H. Duncan, *College Typewriting* (7th ed.; Cincinnati: South-Western Publishing Co., 1965), pp. x + 374.

Lloyd, Alan, and Russell Hosler, *Personal Typing* (New York: McGraw-Hill Book Co., Inc., 1959), pp. viii + 120.

Menzel, Donald H., Howard Jones, and Lyle Boyd, *Writing a Technical Paper* (New York: McGraw-Hill Book Co., Inc., 1961), pp. ix + 132.

Wanous, S. J., *Statistical Typing* (Cincinnati: South-Western Publishing Co., 1965), p. 62.

Winfrey, Robley, *Technical and Business Report Preparation* (3rd ed.; Ames, Iowa: Iowa State University Press, 1962), pp. x + 340.

chapter 16
editing the manuscript

All manuscripts must be edited. The process of checking the contents for accuracy, completeness, clarity, and conformity with standards can improve them substantially. It is desirable to have another person review your manuscript as well. A good checklist for use in editing follows in Figure 19. Figure 20 presents a series of sound questions to raise and answer in the course of editing.

CONTENTS

Fulfillment of purpose

Accuracy and completeness

    background material
    scope defined
    numerical data
    tables and charts
    quotations
    examples and explanations
    facts and other evidence
    duplication
    repetition
    irrelevant material
    conclusions

Main issues

Minor issues

Logical development

Flow of ideas

Emphasis

MECHANICAL CORRECTNESS

English

    spelling
    punctuation
    grammar

Form

    type of report
    parts of report
    margins
    paragraphing
    footnote form
    bibliographical form
    subject headings
    consistency

Figure 19

AN EDITORIAL CHECKLIST FOR MANUSCRIPTS

Source: Leland Brown, *Effective Business Report Writing* (Englewood Cliffs, New Jersey: Prentice-Hall, Inc., 1955), p. 193.

Figure 19 (Cont'd.)

ORGANIZATION

Overall

Relationship of parts

Position of topics

Sequence of ideas

Transition

Unity

smooth phrasing
use of topic sentences

Words

concrete
familiar
precise
simple
abstract concepts defined

CLEARNESS OF EXPRESSION

Sentences

specific facts and details
varied sentence structure
short sentences predominant
average sentence length
grammatically correct sentences

ADAPTATION TO READER

Level of readability

Tone

Experience and knowledge

Interest

I a. Has my paper (chapter) a single informing theme, with its proper developments, or is it merely a series of loosely connected ideas and images?

b. Does my beginning begin and does my conclusion conclude? (A beginning should not go back to the Flood, and a conclusion is not the same thing as a summing up.)

c. Is each of my paragraphs a division with a purpose; that is, does it organize a number of sentences into a treatment of one idea and its modifications?

d. Is each sentence contrived to stand on its own feet or is it thrown off balance by the load of qualifiers or the drag of afterthoughts?

e. Have I made proper use of transitional words and phrases to keep all my connections clear? E.g., nevertheless, moreover, even, still, of course (in its use of minimizing the idea before), to be sure, admittedly, etc. (The transitional word or phrase is usually better in the course of the sentence than at the beginning.)

Figure 20

QUESTIONS TO ASK IN WRITING AND REVISING

Source: Reprinted from *The Modern Researcher* by Jacques Barzun and Henry F. Graff, copyright © 1957, by Jacques Barzun. By permission of Harcourt, Brace & World, Inc.

Figure 20 (Cont'd.)

II a. What is the <u>tone</u> of my piece? Is it too stiff and too formal, trying for the effect of authority? Is it perhaps too relaxed, too familiar, too facetious? Or is it, as it should be, simple, direct?

b. Are there any passages that I especially prize? If so, am I sure that, in my creative enthusiasm, I am not delighted with something "fancy"?

c. Have I been conscious of the reader and have I consulted his convenience? Or have I, on the contrary, been easy only on myself and used a "private" language?

d. Could I, if called upon to do so, explain the exact meaning and function of every word I have used? E.g., <u>subjective</u>, <u>objective</u>, <u>significant</u>, <u>realistic</u>, <u>impact</u>, <u>value</u>.

e. Are my metaphors aids to the reader or merely ways for me to escape my own difficulty?

III a. Is it perfectly clear to which noun or noun-clause my pronouns refer? (The slightest ambiguity is fatal.)

b. Have I tried to give an air of judicious reserve by repeating the words <u>somewhat</u>, <u>rather</u>, <u>perhaps</u>, and have I used for this purpose the illiterate "to an extent"? Or, conversely, have I overdone the emphatic with <u>very</u>, <u>invariably</u>, <u>tremendous</u>, <u>extraordinary</u>, and the like?

c. Have I arbitrarily broken or altered the idiomatic links between certain words, particularly between verbs and their allied prepositions, committing such solecisms as: <u>disagree</u> . . . <u>to</u>, <u>equally</u> . . . <u>as</u>, <u>prefer</u> . . . <u>than</u>?

d. Have I imported from sciences and disciplines in which I am interested a vocabulary out of place in civilized writing? What jargon and vogue words have slipped out by force of habit? Examples of jargon are: <u>integrate</u>, <u>area</u>, <u>finalize</u>, <u>frame of reference</u>, <u>methodology</u>, <u>in terms of</u>, <u>level</u> <u>approach</u>, etc.

e. Have I preferred the familiar word to the farfetched? the concrete to the abstract? the single to the circumlocution? the short to the long?

In revising a draft you may have inadvertently repeated identical information in different parts of your manuscript. Occasionally such repetition is permissible, but it should be phrased differently. A review of the text frequently discloses lack of information, inadequate treatment of a key point, or overemphasis on relatively unimportant material. Although few authors like to discard the results of hard work, it is sometimes necessary to delete extraneous material that may detract from the merits of the remainder.

Rereading a manuscript frequently discloses to the author the words, phrases, or sentences that are unclear, meaningless, pretentious, wordy, trite, or awkward. With the aid of a grammar book, dictionary, and thesaurus you can remedy such weaknesses.

To transpose from one part of a page to another draw a circle around the passage, draw a line to the margin, then continue the line to a caret (.) below the desired point of insertion. To transfer from one page to another, draw a circle around the passage on page 21, for example, and write in the margin "insert A p. 20." On page 20 write "tr A from p. 21," circle this note, and connect it to the caret at the desired insertion point.

Manuscripts are first printed in galleys (long, unbroken columns of type), proofs of which are corrected; then they are divided into pages. Page proofs provide the final opportunity for correction.

Bibliography

Blickle, Margaret, and Kenneth Houp, *Reports for Science and Industry* (New York: Henry Holt and Co., 1958), pp. x + 320.

Bromage, Mary, *Writing for Business* (Ann Arbor, Michigan: University of Michigan Press, 1965), pp. xii + 178.

Comer, David, III, and Ralph Spillman, *Modern Technical and Industrial Reports* (New York: G. P. Putnam's Sons, 1962), pp. xix + 425.

Guam, Carl, Harold Graves, and Lyne Hoffman, *Report Writing* (3rd ed.; New York: Prentice-Hall, Inc., 1950), pp. xv + 384.

Gunning, Robert, *New Guide to More Effective Writing in Business and Industry* (Boston; Industrial Education Institute, 1962), p. 332.

Ulman, Joseph, Jr., and Jay Gould, *Technical Reporting* (New York: Henry Holt and Co., 1959), pp. vii + 382.

Williams, Cecil, and John Ball, *College Writing* (New York: Ronald Press Co., 1957), pp. xix + 475.

Winfrey, Robley, *Technical and Business Report Preparation* (3rd ed.; Ames, Iowa: Iowa State University Press, 1962), pp. x + 340.

chapter 17
coordinating content

Each chapter or section of the report, thesis, or dissertation must be designed for a specific purpose. These subdivisions can be considered custom-designed building blocks. In evaluating the work, however, we look not only at the individual blocks but also at the overall structure. Any criticism of a chapter is based upon its dual nature as a self-contained treatment and as a contributing member of the total structure.

The "total structure" consists of the chapters proper and two supporting elements: the *front matter*, which precedes Chapter 1, and the *back matter*, which follows the final chapter.

This chapter is devoted to specifying what ought to be included in the chapters and in their supporting front and back materials. An overall view of the entire work usually contains the elements listed in Figure 21, although some of them are optional, depending upon their necessity in a specific report and the requirements of the educational institution for which it is written.

FRONT MATTER

Blank sheet

Title page

Dedication (optional)

Preface (optional)

Abstract

Table of contents

List of tables (if any)

List of figures (graphs and illustrations, if any)

List of cases (if any)

List of appendixes (if any)

Figure 21

ELEMENTS OF A THESIS

Figure 21 (Cont'd.)

TEXT PROPER

Introduction or Chapter 1

Body of the work (as many chapters as are necessary to present the data)

Summary, conclusions, and recommendations

BACK MATTER

Appendixes (if any)

Glossary (if any)

Bibliography

Index (optional)

Blank sheet

Front Matter

Title Page. The preferred format of the title page varies slightly from one university to another, but what it includes is fairly standard: the title itself, which should be as brief as possible; your name and most recent academic degree; the nature of the work and the class or purpose for which it is submitted; the date; and for graduate papers the name of the university. Figure 22 is an example of such a title page, but it is best to consult the specific departmental requirements of your own institution.

Dedication. A dedication is optional. If you decide to include one, keep it brief (less than three lines long), dignified, and unsentimental: for example, "This thesis is dedicated to Dr. Robert L. Fraser. His patient, sound, and willing advice guided and immeasurably facilitated this research effort."

Preface. The preface is an informal personal statement. It thus differs from the other parts of the manuscript in which your research and conclusions are presented more formally and impersonally. The preface is the place to explain why you chose the topic and the specific approach, to describe whatever benefits you may have obtained from the research and writing, and to set forth the purpose of the study and describe the limits that you have imposed. It is also the place to express gratitude for the assistance of others if it is appropriate.

You may wish to include a brief summary of your own background and experience if it is germane and to suggest how your manuscript can be useful in future work by yourself and others.

The preface should be brief, preferably only one page long and not more than two. It should be concise, factual, and tactful. It should be dated and signed. The date goes at the left-hand margin one inch below the last line; your name goes at the right-hand margin on the same line as the date. The title is

---

MANAGEMENT STRUCTURE IN THE PLASTICS INDUSTRY

by

Albert Edward Hoover, B.A.
Harvard University

Thesis submitted in partial fulfillment
of the requirements for the degree

of

Master of Business Administration

New York University
June 1969

Figure 22

A SAMPLE TITLE PAGE FOR A THESIS

---

simply "preface," typed in capitals and centered 1 1/2 inches below the top edge of the paper. The text of the preface should start four lines below the title.

The preface is optional; many manuscripts, reports in particular, do not have prefaces, although short prefatory notes of a few sentences are permissible.

Abstract. The abstract is a summary of the manuscript. It is entitled "Abstract of [title of work]"; this heading is typed in capitals and centered 1 1/2 inches from the top edge of the page.

The abstract should not be a detailed report. It should simply provide the reader with a general idea of the content of the manuscript so that he can determine whether or not it is necessary to read the entire work. It contains a statement of the problem and the hypothesis tested, a description of the purpose of the study, an outline of the approach, and a summary of the results. In most instances it mentions all chapter or section contents.

The abstract for a thesis will be only a page or two long; dissertation abstracts are frequently limited to 500 words but may be longer. In a report the abstract should include, in addition to the material already listed, a summary of recommendations for action. The length of such an abstract depends upon the length of the report. One authority suggests that between 1 and 10 percent of the number of words in the manuscript is a reasonable length.[1] See Figure 23 for an example.

ABSTRACT OF [title of work]

The concept of union participation in corporate management is neither unique nor new in this country. From time to time the cry for such participation is renewed from some quarter. Proponents of this idea believe that compulsory participation would be the best method for settling labor disputes and would provide an effective guarantee of industrial peace. This thesis is concerned with the problem of whether or not compulsory participation could actually be effective in maintaining labor peace in the United States.

Such a study is significant because the enactment of compulsory-participation laws would completely alter the present system of capitalistic free enterprise in the United States. The role of government in labor-management relations would be greatly increased, and the present relationship between management and labor would be considerably altered.

Research data were collected from Federal and state laws, law journals, periodicals, magazine and newspaper articles, textbooks, and research reports on various aspects of the problem. The study included a review of laws relating to mediation and union participation in management enacted by various foreign governments.

An attempt to study and present a balanced sample of laws, arguments, opinions, and ideas was made. There was no attempt, however, to describe every such law enacted or every opinion or argument voiced on the subject.

Figure 23

A SAMPLE ABSTRACT

---

[1]Frank Kerekes and Robley Winfrey, *Report Preparation—Including Correspondence and Technical Writing* (2nd ed.; Ames, Iowa: Iowa State College Press, 1951), p. 312.

Figure 23 (Cont'd.)

The study was designed to test the hypothesis that compulsory participation cannot work effectively to prevent labor disputes in the United States.

The research was aimed at four aspects. Chapter 2 deals with Federal legislation relating to mediation, conciliation, and arbitration, in order to determine how the Federal government dealt with labor-management disputes. Chapter 3 describes union-participation legislation enacted by foreign nations, in order to present comparative material. The difficulties confronted by these nations in enforcing the laws have also been reviewed.

Chapter 4 treats the arguments for and against increased government intervention, in an attempt to determine their respective validity. It also includes a study of compulsory participation. . . .

Table of Contents. The form of the table of contents is well defined. Note the following specifications (see Figure 24 for a sample content):

1. The title, "Table of Contents" or simply "Contents," is centered in capitals 1 1/2 inches from the top edge of the paper. The front matter preceding the table of contents (preface, abstract, and so on) need not be included. If you do include it, follow instructions for back matter given later in this chapter.

2. Two line spaces below the title type the word "Page" at the right-hand margin. Lists of tables, figures, and the like are entered at the left-hand margin two line spaces lower. If there are no such lists "Chapter" is placed at the left-hand margin on the same line as "Page."

3. The chapter by chapter content of your work comes next. The question usually arises as to the extent of detail to place in this section. Generally, only chapter headings and first-order subheadings are included. It is a good idea to type the table of contents after you have typed the body of the work, so that you can be sure that the headings are exactly the same. Even though your chapters may contain more headings, for example, third order and fourth order, they should usually be omitted from the table of contents; including them would make the table too long, and reduce its clarity and utility. The Index is the place that provides *all* the significant topics and headings for the reader.

4. The important words in both chapter and subordinate headings have initial capitals only. First-order subheads are indented two letter spaces from the chapter headings.

5. Single-space between all subheadings within one chapter; double-space between chapters, that is, between the last subheading of one chapter and the following chapter heading; double-space between each chapter heading and the first subheading that follows it; double-space between all front-matter and back-matter titles.

6. Chapter headings are given Arabic numbers. Headings that require more than one line are single-spaced and aligned at the left, without indentation.

7. The titles of the back matter are capitalized. The major subsections of the Bibliography, for example, List of Books and List of Articles, are inserted in the Table of Contents as are first-order subheadings of a chapter.

8. The *only* terminal punctuation used in the entire table of contents is the periods after the chapter numbers.

9. All headings, subheadings, and so forth should employ a consistent grammatical structure. Do not, for example, title one subheading "Entry into Consumer Markets" while you name the other "Entering Industrial Markets."

TABLE OF CONTENTS

Figure 24

A SAMPLE TABLE OF CONTENTS

Lists of Tables, Figures, Cases, and Appendixes. All the tables, figures, cases and appendixes included in your work must be listed, each category on a separate page. The titles in the lists should be identical with those in the manuscript. The format of each list is similar to that of the table of contents.

An example of a List of Tables is presented in Figure 25, Sample List of Tables. The format for Figures, Cases, and Appendixes is identical. The specifications to be noted for constructing such lists follow. Refer to Figure 25 for conformance with each specification.

1. The heading, "List of Tables" (or Figures, etc.), is centered and typed in caps 1 1/2 inches from the top edge of the paper.

2. Two line spaces below the title type "Table" (or "Figure," "Case,"

"Appendix") at the left margin in initial caps; type "Page" at the right margin in initial caps.

3. Skip two spaces and begin entering the table numbers, titles, and pages. Single-space for titles requiring more than one line; double-space between separate items in the list.

4. No periods are used after the numbers, titles, or page numbers.

5. Regardless of how many pages are taken up by a table, it is only the *first* page that is cited.

LIST OF TABLES*

Table		Page
1	The Manufacturers of Polyethylene	17
2	Salesmen's Compensation, by Territories, for Five Major Plastics Manufacturers	29
3	The Sale of Plastic Film, by States, in 1966	42
4	Grades and Sizes of Polyethylene Film Sold in the United States, 1966	71

*The formats for Figures, Cases, and Appendixes are identical.

Figure 25

A SAMPLE LIST OF TABLES

Text

First Chapter. The first chapter is quite formal, for it must fulfill certain standard functions. Its main objective is to orient the reader to the purpose of the manuscript, to define its scope, to review the relevant literature, to suggest the significance of the study, and so on. When the reader finishes Chapter 1 he must understand what the author is trying to do so that he can properly evaluate all that is presented subsequently.

The introductory chapter is usually eight to fifteen pages long. It should contain the following seven parts, each clearly distinguished and in this sequence: title (often simply "Introduction" is most appropriate); objectives (a few paragraphs on the specific purpose of the study, including a statement of the hypothesis and, in a business report, when and by whom the report was authorized); significance (here, the writer explains *why* the study is important). Simply stated, he should answer the question "Why should anyone take the trouble to guide him or to read and evaluate the completed manuscript?" He must justify the effort that has been expended in terms of the work's value to students, scholars, business enterprises, government agencies, society, or the like.

The student is expected to indicate what other investigators have done. This applies not only to those investigators who have done research on the precise objective that the student intends to pursue, but also applies to those whose work is relevant because it sheds some light, no matter how little, on the objective. This prior research can be examined in several ways: by elucidation of its strengths and weaknesses; by dividing it into useful categories such as historical periods, economic philosophies, or geographic areas; by drawing analogies from other fields; and by comparison with any number of useful criteria.

The value of each of the previous research efforts must be stated in terms which show how this prior work can contribute to the proposed work. The writer must not only show that he is intimately familiar with what has been done earlier, but explain why the present study is necessary and in what ways it goes beyond and adds to previous work.

The student may be able to present this section in several pages; some subjects, however, may require as many as ten pages. This is *not* the place for *protracted* analysis and argument about prior work, but merely the place to review briefly and present a "gestalt" (a unified whole) or overview which points up the value of the present work.

Once the literature review has been completed, the next logical section should specify the scope and limits of the study—a definition of *your* precise contribution and your reasons for selecting the specific limitations on intensity, period, locale, historical or conceptual categories, age groups, and so on; limitations on the applicability of your research should also be clarified.

By presenting the limitations, the writer also explains what he does *not* propose to do in the area studied. For example, in studying the job induction practices of chemical firms, limits may be set that confine the study only to those firms with sales of $50,000,000 or less. Time limitations are readily cited by referring to the chronological boundaries of the research design. Thus, an analysis of the dividend policies of electric power corporations, based on their Annual Reports for the years 1958 through 1968, pinpoints the range in years of the study.

There are limits of another type, however, which relate to the *applicability* of the data, for example, the sample treated in a survey may be too small to be more than illustrative of an approach and not definitive. Or, the results may be validly applied only to a small community in Northern Maine. These then, are limits of *use* as opposed to the limits of the breadth of the work that were illustrated in the previous paragraph.

The limitations of the report, thesis, or dissertation are, in large part, the responsibility of the student. It is the student who sets them after examining the prior work in the field, the data available to him, the time, money, and skill that he possesses, the needs and opportunities of the discipline, and the standards of his university. Whatever the limits are that the student sets, they must be reasonable ones. Often, one page will suffice for this section. A representative page showing the scope and limits of a study is presented in Figure 26.

SCOPE AND LIMITS

This study will attempt to examine the product manager system. Its scope will be confined to organizational structure and relationships, training requirements, compensation, responsibility, and performance evaluation techniques. Thus, the investigation's findings should permit a reader to answer such questions as: What is a product manager? Is his compensation appropriate to his training and responsibilities? Can we accurately evaluate the quality and quantity of his performance? And so forth.

The work will be limited to companies in a single industry so that it can be properly performed in the scheduled time and with the modest budget available. For this purpose the chemical industry was selected. In addition, only those chemical firms will be studied that have annual sales of $10 million or more, and a minimum product management staff of three people.

Figure 26

AN EXAMPLE OF SCOPE AND LIMITS SECTION OF A STUDY

This section on *procedure* tells the reader precisely *what* is going to be done by the writer. It should start out by discussing the type of data and how they will be obtained (for example, experimental data obtained by telephone interviewing), the amount of data (for example, interviews with twenty manufacturers of ball-point pens), and the time schedule for the work. If special libraries or literature resources are to be used they should be noted. If the research is going to depend upon journal articles found by searching certain indexes, this must be explicitly stated. Definitions of terms or concepts not customary in the literature of the field or used in a special way by the writer must be succinctly and accurately defined. For example, the term "small business" is open to several interpretations and must be carefully defined.

When research designs must be outlined, questionnaires presented and analyzed, laboratory diagrams shown, and the like, it is customary to put such material in a separate chapter on "experimental procedures" or "research design." It is also customary to give the reader some idea of the organization and treatment of the remaining chapters, so that he can see the relationship of each part to the whole work. A good way to do it is in a series of paragraphs, one for each chapter, describing clearly but generally what it will cover. Thus, the paragraph for Chapter 3 might state:

Chapter 3—Geographic Location of Polyethylene Producers—will set forth the location economics of existing polyethylene plants. At the same time, it will discuss those factors critical to locating new plants and will forecast the probable location of similar plants built in the next year, and so forth. Information will be obtained from trade journals and from personal interviews with executives of all of the top ten polyethylene manufacturers.

Once a student has decided upon a topic, he should prepare a prospectus for the instructor's review, comment, and approval. The object of the prospectus is to "sell" the instructor on the merits of the topic, its scope, the approach, and so on. He will approve the topic only if its value is clear.

As the prospectus has been highly structured, it is often useful as an outline for the first chapter. Beside saving the student some time, use of the standard form for Chapter 1 helps to direct the writer's thinking and preliminary research. The specific requirements for the introductory chapter serve to channel the energies of the student and to establish criteria for evaluating his work.

For a thesis or dissertation the prospectus itself must include a timetable, listing the approximate dates when each part of the work will have been completed and submitted to the adviser:

Work	Schedule
outline	September 30
bibliography (mailing of questionnaire)	October 31
Chapter 1 (introduction, field interviews, coding of replies to questionnaire)	November 30
Chapter 2 (analysis of replies to questionnaire and results of field interviews)	January 15
Chapter 3	February 15
Chapter 4	March 15
. . .	
final chapter (summary, conclusions, and recommendations)	April 1
front matter and back matter	April 10
first draft typed	May 1
final draft typed	May 15
perfect copy submitted	May 25

In addition, all critical steps (mailing of questionnaires, coding, analyzing replies, setting up laboratory equipment, conducting tests or interviews, and so on) should be specified in the timetable.

The Body of the Manuscript. This major portion of the work can be organized in many ways: according to the field of the research; the method of study; the type, quantity, and quality of data; the writer's style. No matter how it is organized, it should be factually accurate, clearly argued, succinctly written, grammatically correct—and clearly bearing the hallmarks of a serious effort by the student to lay the cornerstone of his career in higher education.

There are, however, a few principles that can help in organizing the work. First, five chapters (not counting the first and final chapters) are usually enough. Second, one of these chapters should be devoted to a detailed critical analysis of the "state of the art." Sometimes two or three chapters will have to be devoted to such analysis, perhaps one for each trend of thought, historical period, geographical area, and so on. Third, one chapter should be devoted to explanation and justification of method: experimental techniques, analytical devices, research design, questionnaire, or whatever has been necessary. Fourth, at least one chapter should ordinarily be devoted to presentation of your own research findings, including tables, equations, formulas, statistical analyses, and comprehensive description of your work. This part of the work would be developed at length in a dissertation but dealt with more summarily in a report. Finally, one chapter should be devoted to comparison of your findings with those described in your critical analysis of earlier work. This comparison must be a critical one, a thorough and objective assessment of your work in the light of what other researchers have done. Points of similarity and difference should be highlighted.

Each chapter in the body of the work should begin with a brief introduction, setting forth your plan for that chapter. A half-page will ordinarily suffice for this introduction. In addition, it should end with a brief summary of what it has accomplished. Once again, a half-page or slightly more, will suffice in most cases.

The length of the chapters is variable, depending upon the nature, quality, quantity, and so on of the work and your approach. Some chapters may be eight to ten pages long, others thirty or more. The entire body of a master's thesis usually ranges from 40 to 100 pages. A dissertation generally ranges from 150 to 300 pages.

Final Chapter. The final chapter logically includes an overall summary of the work and the author's conclusions and recommendations. As such, it is often entitled "Summary, Conclusions, and Recommendations."

The summary section should be clearly labeled. It differs from the summaries at the end of each previous chapter in that it embraces the *entire* work, from its original conception as set forth in the introduction, but is less specific in details. Only the major elements of the work should be stated, together with the reasons for that particular treatment. Less important details should remain *only* in the summaries of the individual chapters in the body of the manuscript.

Every researcher *must* draw conclusions from his research findings, even though they may not be the ones that he originally hoped for and expected. (Negative results may be of tremendous value and are a legitimate contribution to knowledge.) It is crucial that he demonstrate his ability to interpret such findings succinctly and unambiguously, weighing his approach against others that might have been taken. Indeed such a demonstration is the point of the whole undertaking. As the work will be read by people who are expert in the field, it also is far less embarrassing when the student shows his awareness of any shortcomings.

If the research has been well done, the student should be able to make recommendations. The nature and penetration of his presentation here will provide the reader with a direct measure of the quality of his research. It does not really matter whether or not the research has been successful in proving or disproving an hypothesis; if acceptable techniques have been intelligently and carefully applied, the author should be able to make sound suggestions to other scholars for further research, to business firms that can use the findings, to government agencies, to trade associations, and so on.

The final chapter is usually about six to ten pages long in a thesis and about ten to fifteen pages long in a dissertation.

See Figure 27 for an example of each of the three parts of the final chapter.

SUMMARY

In this report on product abandonment, the initial hypothesis was that a product-abandonment model could be constructed. The primary task of this paper was then to formulate such a model and to test it.

The first step in construction of the model was a thorough study of the literature on the abandonment of products, facilities, plants, communities, and so on, from the perspectives of economics, management, marketing, accounting, psychology, and politics. To facilitate treatment of the literature, as well as to set the stage for subsequent development of the abandonment model, the results of this survey were classified in several categories.

In the first category, the approaches of the accountant, the economist, the sales manager, and the government agency to abandonment situations were examined. . . . It was shown that, although each point of view has some merit, it is nevertheless too narrow, neglecting some factors and dismissing others that are of primary importance in other points of view. The conclusion was that each view has some merit but none will alone permit a thorough analysis of abandonment situations. A perspective drawing upon several points of view seems necessary to guarantee such comprehensive examination. . . .

Figure 27

A SAMPLE OF THE FINAL CHAPTER

Figure 27 (Cont'd.)

CONCLUSIONS

Several principal conclusions may be drawn. First, the product-abandonment model has been successfully tested; it is practical and can be an invaluable guide to crucial decisions. It ensures that all the many factors—tangible and intangible, quantitative and qualitative—relevant to an abandonment decision are included in a coherent and unified structure.

Second, the decision model developed can serve as a guide to the analyst; it is a tool that he can use to determine the relative desirability of certain decisions. Compelling strategic factors may, however, dictate decisions contrary to those logically indicated by the model. . . .

RECOMMENDATIONS

As a result of this study, these specific recommendations can be made to management. First, general abandonment policies should be formulated by business organizations in terms that will serve as a guide to action in specific instances. Second, management should familiarize itself with the existing network of regulations and restraints that operate in the area of abandonment, that is, with the actual and potential effects of "organized intervention." As enforced recognition of the firm's social obligations is thoroughly undesirable, management should structure its present and future abandonment policies to reduce pressure for organized control over abandonment. This effort may necessitate another look at the policies of inaction pursued at present and even a vigorous attack upon the growing network of organized interference. . . .

Back Matter

Appendix. An appendix, as its name implies is a section *added* to the main part of the manuscript; it follows immediately after the final chapter. This "extra" character does not mean that it is not useful; it should fill an important function in the total work. The appendix should contain material that is crucial enough to be included in the manuscript but too detailed to form part of the body of the work. Placing such material at the end permits a more immediate comprehension of the central issues yet provides an opportunity for extended examination of subsidiary data as required. Copies of letters and questionnaires; texts of court decisions, government regulations, company policy statements, and the like; the derivations of statistical or mathematical formulas and sample calculations; tables, graphs, and illustrations too complex for the body of the work (tabulations of consumer purchasing power by city and state, for example) or not of primary relevance to the study; and samples of forms (for example, purchase orders and checklists of interview questions) used in constructing the treatise are generally collected in the appendixes.

Reference should be made in the text, usually in a footnote, to any material in the appendixes.

There can be more than one appendix. In that event each is usually identified by a capital letter: Appendix A, Appendix B, and so on. Each appendix begins on a new page, just as does each chapter, and is listed by letter and title in the table of contents.

The material within each appendix is arranged in the order in which it is referrred to in the text.

Glossary. A glossary is an alphabetical list of terms, especially technical terms or abbreviations, requiring definition. The need for a glossary does not arise until· there are a dozen or so items that require explanation. It is placed immediately following the appendixes (or the final chapter if there are not appendixes). The word "Glossary" should be in caps, centered, and positioned 1 1/2 inches from the top edge of the page. Each entry in the glossary is defined in *exact* language, clarifying usage that may be unfamiliar or ambiguous to readers. It is a quick and convenient reference tool that eliminates the need for interrupting the text with such explanations. See Figure 28 for a sample glossary.

GLOSSARY OF TERMS

Net Railway Operating Income—The amount left from railway operating revenues after deduction of all expenses, taxes, and rents for equipment and joint facilities.

Ton-Mile—The transportation of one ton of freight one mile, as a unit of measure and pricing.

Gross Ton-Miles per Freight-Train Hour—The number of gross tons of freight-train equipment and contents moved one mile during one hour.

Figure 28

A SAMPLE GLOSSARY OF TERMS

Source: Adapted from *Annual Report, 1966* (New York: New York Central Railroad, 1967), p. 2.

Bibliography. Every manuscript must have a bibliography, a list of *all* the sources cited in both the text and the footnotes, plus others selected for their relevance to the work though not cited directly. The form of a bibliographical entry is different from that of a note because its purpose is different: whereas a note usually gives the *specific* location of certain material within a given publication, the bibliographical entry refers to the source *in general,* to an entire book or article. Furthermore, the bibliography provides an alphabetical listing of all sources in the study, as a convenient tool for other investigators, and therefore the first author's last name is given first in each entry.

The bibliography must include:

1. all works referred to in the text
2. all works referred to in the footnotes
3. additional works selected for their relevance to the study.

Selecting materials for the bibliography requires careful judgment. If *all* relevant works were to be included, the bibliography would often be unwieldy; not *all* relevant works are useful or reliable, and their inclusion would be misleading. Generally, it is wise to select on the basis of *quality.* If you know that you examined but did not cite many widely respected sources, include them in your bibliography, but omit the secondary and other minor sources that add nothing but length to the list. "Padding" a bibliography is a common temptation, but remember that scholars can spot such a practice at a glance.

In addition, if you are dealing with only one aspect of a broad subject, it is important that the bibliography also contain entries for background materials on the larger subject. If you select judiciously, the importance of the whole field and the place of your subject area within it will be clearly visible simply from study of your bibliography.

Although the entries are arranged alphabetically according to the *last* name of the first author, it may be convenient to divide the bibliography into several categories and to alphabetize within each. The following classifications are generally useful for business writing: books, articles, reports and pamphlets, interviews, correspondence, and miscellaneous sources (including newspaper reports, speeches, cases, advertisements, and business articles).

When there is no author's name, it is best to use the first major work of the title to alphabetize the reference.[2] The initial article in the title, as in *The Fundamentals of Production Planning* and *A Look at Organization Theory,* does not control alphabetical placement. The two examples would be alphabetized under "F" and "L" respectively.

If an author is also the first listed coauthor of another publication, the joint work appears after all those of which he is the sole author.

With the minor exceptions noted below, the form of the bibliographical

---

[2]Alternative systems include placing alphabetical listings of publications without authors *before* the list of works alphabetized by author and alphabetizing them in the author list under "anonymous."

references is to be *identical to that specified for the footnotes.* The exceptions are:

The entries are not numbered. The first author's last name is presented first, followed by a comma, then by his first name and any initials, the names of all coauthors, and finally by a comma. In references with two or more authors all but the first have their names listed in the normal order. For books and reports page numbers can generally be omitted entirely, or the total number of pages, including index and all front matter, can be given. For articles, the page numbers of each *entire* article must be given. In most other aspects the bibliographical entry can be identical with the footnote form.

Some authorities prefer other minor modifications in form, for example, using a period instead of a comma after the authors' names and not enclosing the facts of publication in parentheses. However, it is the opinion of the authors and many others that there is nothing to be gained and much time to be lost in changing the form. Students and faculty members alike have enough to do to produce a good manuscript without having to go to unnecessary trouble. For an example of correct bibliographical form, see the reference list at the end of each chapter in this book as well as Figure 29.

BIBLIOGRAPHY

Books

Alderson, Wroe, and Paul E. Green, <u>Planning and Problem Solving in Marketing</u> (Homewood, Illinois: Richard D. Irwin, Inc., 1964), pp. x + 661.

Ferber, Robert, and P. J. Verdoorn, <u>Research Methods in Economics and Business</u> (New York: The Macmillan Co., 1962), pp. xiv + 573.

Greene, James H., <u>Production Control: Systems and Decisions</u> (Homewood, Illinois: Richard D. Irwin, Inc., 1965), pp. xii + 605.

Harper, Donald V., <u>Price Policy and Procedure</u> (New York: Harcourt, Brace & World, 1966), pp. xi + 308.

Articles

Cleland, David I., "Understanding Project Authority", <u>Business Horizons</u> (Spring, 1967), Vol. 10, No. 1, pp. 63-70.

Figure 29

A SAMPLE BIBLIOGRAPHY

Figure 29 (Cont'd.)

Hayes, Samuel L., and Russell A. Taussig, "Tactics of Cash Takeover Bids",
    Harvard Business Review (March-April, 1967), Vol. 45, No. 2,
    pp. 135-148.
Stanton, Frank, "What Is Wrong with Test Marketing"?, Journal of Marketing
    (April, 1967), Vol. 31, No. 2, pp. 43-47.

Reports

Mayer, Kurt B., and Sidney Goldstein, The First Two Years: Problems of
    Small Firm Growth and Survival (Small Business Research Series No. 2;
    Washington, D.C.: Small Business Administration, 1961), pp. x + 233.
O'Meara, J. Roger, Employee Patent and Secrecy Agreements (Personnel Policy
    Study No. 199; New York: National Industrial Conference Board, Inc.,
    1965), p. 94.

Interviews

Brown, Arthur, Vice-President for Business Development, Simpson Chemical Co.,
    New York; July 13, 1967, personal interview.
Hall, Robert, Chief Economist, Hall Tool Company, Newark, N.J., July 12,
    1967, telephone interview.

Correspondence

Benson, George, Vice-President for Marketing, Simpson Chemical Co., New
    York, April 15, 1967; letter to the author.
Benson, George, Vice-President for Marketing, Simpson Chemical Co., New
    York, April 5, 1967; letter to John Deeds, Director of Research,
    Alliance Chemical Co., Pittsburgh, Pa.

Miscellaneous

Borden, Charles, "Product Pricing and Anti-Trust Legislation", paper delivered
    to the 158th National Meeting of the American Chemical Society,
    Los Angeles, California, April 11, 1967.
Hughes, William, "The New Economic System", CBC-TV Network series on
    American Business in 1967, July 15, 1967.

The title "Bibliography" should be centered at the top of the page in capital letters, exactly as are chapter headings, that is, 1 1/2 inches from the top edge. Below this, suitably spaced, centered, and with initial caps, should be the title of the individual category. Each entry begins at the left-hand margin; succeeding lines of each entry should be indented one-half inch (five pica or six elite spaces), so that the alphabetization is prominent. Single-space *within* sources, and double-space *between* them. When two or more works by a single author appear one after the other, you can avoid repeating his name by substituting seven or eight hyphens in all but the first entry. When you list works of which he is first coauthor, however, you must type his name in full again.

Index. The index, located at the very end of the manuscript, is an alphabetical listing of all important topics, subtopics, and names discussed or even mentioned in the text. The manuscript page numbers where each may be found are given. If it is reasonable to assume that a certain topic, place, or the like may be sought by someone, then it should be included in the index.

Writing the Report

The instructions presented in this book so far have been extensive enough for preparing a thesis or dissertation, but a report does not always require the same strict form or such thorough investigation. A report is by definition simply an "account." It is a collection of information designed for use; it may contain a historical record, plans, programs, recommendations for action, and the like. But these facts must be put together in a framework that has two main characteristics:[3]

1. The report must be accurate, complete, clearly and skillfully written, unbiased, logical, and questioning.
2. Although each report has unique contents, its organization and style must adhere to a generally accepted form.

These two characteristics are best served if the student will extract from the comprehensive guide to the preparation of theses and dissertations enough information about the necessary parts of a report so that he can be guided in its preparation.

Most of the instructions contained in this book can be useful in writing reports. But the length is usually limited to between fifteen and twenty pages, so that certain adaptations must be made, mostly condensations. Instead of a chapter-length introduction a page may be enough; the same applies to the summary, conclusions, and recommendations. The abstract, table of contents, preface, index, and so on can be omitted in writing a report.

[3] Leland Brown, *Effective Business Report Writing* (Englewood Cliffs, New Jersey: Prentice-Hall, Inc., 1955), pp. 4-6.

Figure 30 shows an example of a sample paper.

Capitals

VALUE ANALYSIS:
AN AID TO EFFECTIVE ECONOMY PROGRAMS

by

Initial
capitals

Albert Edward Hoover
Management 101, Section C
Professor Harrison T. Fitzgerald
May 14, 1967

Title
Subtitle

VALUE ANALYSIS:
AN AID TO EFFECTIVE ECONOMY PROGRAMS

Definition

Value analysis is the scientific method of securing the same or better performance from a product at the lowest ultimate cost. It is a concentrated effort to improve the value of a product by seeking out and eliminating unnecessary costs

Footnote
citation

whenever they may appear in the cycle of the product design and manufacture.[1]

Unnecessary costs may be eliminated by modifying design or material specifications, by altering the manufacturing process, by changing the source of supply (external or

---

[1] Lawrence D. Miles, "You Can Slash Costs by 25% with Value Analysis", Management Methods (June, 1958), Vol. 14, No. 3, pp. 46-50.

Figure 30

A SAMPLE PAPER

Figure 30 (Cont'd.)

internal), or by eliminating nonfunctional parts or features.[2]

Value analysis necessarily crosses departmental lines; however, since most of the variable product costs are incurred by the purchasing department, it is generally considered a function of that department. It is associated with purchasing department operations; these include cost analysis, interdepartmental cooperation, market analysis, and materials and production analysis.[3]

Objective of Paper

The object of this paper is to set forth the nature of value analysis in sufficient detail for the reader to begin to decide whether such a cost reduction method is useful for his needs. This will be accomplished by describing the nature of the value analysis concept, outlining the steps in a value analysis program, showing the organizational composition and relationships of a value analysis unit, and pointing out some of the results which have been achieved by several firms which have employed this cost-saving program.

Heading

PROCEDURE

Value analysis is a step-by-step procedure in which every product, part, material, and operation in the manufacture of a product is examined. Questions such as the following are asked about each function:

Does the use of this part make the product work better or sell better? Very often it is found that some parts may be eliminated without any loss to the product being manufactured.

Does it perform the needed functions? If a given part,

---

[2] Productive Purchasing (New York: General Electric Corp., 1959), p. 7.

[3] Cutting Costs by Analyzing Values: A Practical Purchasing Program (New York: National Association of Purchasing Agents, 1963), p. 3.

171

Figure 30 (Cont'd.)

material, or operation is not performing its needed function adequately, it should be replaced.

Can we produce it at a lower cost than the firm is currently paying? After allocating all essential costs for a new process to produce a part or material, it may be found there is still a substantial saving over the price that it is paying. In such case, it is advisable to consider making the necessary provisions for the manufacture of the item.

Is its cost proportionate to its usefulness? The cost of some parts may not be proportionate to their usefulness in assembly. In many cases, parts may be eliminated by changing materials or by minor modifications in product design.

Does the item need all of its features? In one instance, stainless steel washers were chamfered (an oblique surface cut on the edge or corner) on one side. This particular operation utilized 70,000 washers per year at 18¢ each. A study revealed that for the indicated use, the chamfer made no contribution to value. By its elimination, the cost was reduced to 5¢ per unit, thereby saving 72 percent of $9,100 each year.[4]

Can it be made by a lower cost method? Several parts which otherwise might have to be assembled can be produced as a casting, thereby eliminating an assembly operation and simplifying production.

Can a standard product be found which will be usable? In some instances, a specially designed part may be eliminated by the use of a standard product, at a substantially lower cost. Even in the case where the use of a standard part requires minor product redesign, it might be found that the overall savings are more than compensating for the redesign expense.

The value specialist must talk to scientists, buyers, and engineers in order to learn what new, low cost materials can be substituted without sacrificing quality. He enlists the ideas of specialty vendors, or gives them suggestions for reducing their own production costs. Meeting with manufacturing men to investigate new tools and processes, he makes sure that the

---

[4] Ibid.

Figure 30 (Cont'd.)

new improvements being proposed are practicable from the manufacturing standpoint.[5]

Since the value analyst is "loosely attached" to a depart-ment, he need not be interrupted with daily duties and inter-departmental problems.[6]

STEPS IN THE VALUE ANALYSIS PROGRAM

Although there are many possible value analysis techniques, the following seven-step "Value Analysis Job Plan" has been successfully implemented.[7]

Subheading

1. Evaluation Phase. The value analyst secures all facts pertinent to costs, quantities, vendors, drawings, specifica-tions, planning, and manufacturing methods. He discusses the facts with engineers and others connected with the product, to secure a better understanding of the problem.

2. Speculative Phase. Every person who may be of assis-tance is consulted, even though some may not be associated with the product. Ideas, suggestions, and possibilities are recorded. Materials processes and parts arrangements are explored. Many believe this stage to be the most important one, although the importance of all phases must be recognized, since it is here that potential solutions are generated. Every suggestion which seems even remotely plausible should be recorded in minute detail. A mind pregnant with ideas can give birth to many money saving possibilities.

---

[5] Miles, op. cit., p. 48.

[6] John Howard Westing and I. V. Fine, Industrial Purchasing: Buying for Industry and Budgetary Institutions (New York: John Wiley and Sons, Inc., 1955), pp. 273-275.

[7] Adapted from the General Electric Plan cited in "Value Analysis", Purchasing (June, 1950), Vol. 28, No. 6, p. 6.

Figure 30 (Cont'd.)

3. <u>Analytical Phase.</u> Each of the ideas recorded in the pre-ceding phase should now be carefully evaluated for practica-bility and consequent money saving. A program might be set up to pursue each idea as vigorously as possible.

4. <u>Vendor Contact Phase.</u> The list of vendors is re-examined. A further search is made for the most suitable suppliers. Suggestions of vendors may be extremely beneficial to the program.

5. <u>Engineering Study Phase.</u> Each suggestion should be analyzed, with the engineers, for practicability and engineering suitability. Many new and valuable suggestions are generated during this phase.

6. <u>Engineering and Vendor Study Phase.</u> The engineer and the vendor are brought together for a final analysis of all of the available possibilities. Changes, trial parts, methods, and tests are suggested with an eye toward lower costs. Each promising suggestion should be tested and retested until tangible results are in evidence.

7. <u>Status Summary and Conclusion.</u> A report containing the results of these steps should be issued. It should encompass the status of each part and the problems in purchasing, man-ufacturing and engineering and should be sent to all interested parties.

Heading   <u>AUTHORITY OF THE VALUE ANALYST</u>

The value specialist acts only in an advisory capacity. In no case does he make decisions with respect to particular products and processes. His job is to supply information that will lead to more profitable decisions by those responsible.

Although value analysis crosses departmental lines, it is usually considered part of the purchasing department. How-

Figure 30 (Cont'd.)

ever, it may correctly be considered part of either the Production or Engineering Departments. The "Value Team" must be available to all departments which can profitably employ their services. In contrast to a part-time operation as a cost reduction program, value analysis is a full-time, continuous operation. It should be noted, however, that at no time does it supersede cost reduction by departments, but merely supplements their efforts.[8]

ORGANIZATION OF THE VALUE ANALYSIS UNIT

The value analysis group is usually small, depending on the size of the company; it may be composed of one to three men and a secretary.

No matter how large the unit, value analysis personnel should possess the following characteristics:[9]

1. Engineering, methods and planning experience, or the equivalent, supported by a general understanding of the properties and uses of materials.

2. A creative imagination.

3. Enough initiative, self-organization, and self-drive to start and complete a task with little or no supervision.

4. An appreciation of the importance of value.

5. Mature, stable, and not easily discouraged.

6. Usually from three to thirty years experience. Since value analysis is based upon realism and not upon theory, actual experience best qualifies a man to grow in this work.

7. The ability and desire to work well with others. Unless many of these situations are skillfully handled, jurisdictional problems and personality clashes arise.

We must never lose sight of the fact that the value analyst acts only in an advisory capacity and makes no product decisions on his own. For this reason, the analyst may not claim credit for the improvements. This credit goes to those

---

[8] Miles, op. cit., p. 47.

[9] Productive Purchasing, op. cit., pp. 3-5.

Figure 30 (Cont'd.)

who review his evaluation results, do the testing, and make the actual decisions.

RESULTS

The results of value analysis have been extremely favorable.[10] The General Electric Company, for example, finds that a value analyst will return $10 to $15 for each dollar of his cost (that is, the cost of training, selection and allocated operation costs).[11]

One should not get the opinion that value analysis benefits only the larger companies; small companies benefit from its use proportionately just as do the larger companies. Some small companies have reported savings from 1 percent to 3 percent of the total purchase cost.[12]

In one firm, a pen-starter and bulb assembly was being purchased for $39.53 per 100. Value analysis revealed that if the assembly were purchased in components, and if material substitutions were made, the assembly could be made at the plant at a projected cost of $14.98 per 100—a saving of $4,500 a year. Similarly, it was brought to the attention of the buyer that the price—six dollars each—of screen covers for synchronous generators might be excessive. The buyer agreed and, working with a value analyst, carefully examined the function of the cover, which was made from expanded metal spot-welded to a steel frame. Consultations with marketing and

---

[10] Howard T. Lewis and Wilbur B. Englund, Procurement: Principles and Cases (Homewood, Illinois: Richard D. Irwin, Inc., 1957), pp. 172-176.

[11] Edward T. Thomson, "The Cost-Cutting Urges", Fortune (March, 1958), Vol. 57, No. 3, p. 120.

[12] Burke B. Cochran, Jr., "Value Analysis in the Smaller Company", Purchasing (September, 1955), Vol. 39, No. 3, pp. 86-88. See also "Does Value Analysis Pay in the Smaller Company?", Purchasing (May, 1957), Vol. 42, No. 5, pp. 74-75.

Figure 30 (Cont'd.)

engineering resulted in redesigning the cover as one-piece stamping, using a perforated die. The cost was reduced to $1.20 each; a yearly saving of $18,500.

Summary and
Conclusions

CONCLUSIONS

Value analysis contributions may be summarized as follows:

1. Cost reduction is effected by purchasing research, such as analysis of price-curves, supply demand relationships, and company experience.

2. Material inventory reduction may be effected by analysis of the economy and of internal operations. The most economic lot sizes are recommended based upon consumption experience, lead time required, and analysis of costs of acquisition and storage.

3. Cost reduction is brought about by analysis of vendor's prices.

4. Production economies are generated by changing the design of the product or the process by which the product is made. These changes may result from investigation of materials, tolerances, physical dimensions, performance requirements.

5. Interdepartmental cooperation is fostered.

6. A more thorough knowledge of basic materials, processes, and costs is required.

7. Management becomes value analysis indoctrinated.[13]

No firm is in a position to ignore the economies that may be instituted through value analysis. Whether it be a part-time operation, or more preferably a full-time specialized area, value analysis can revise the company's present financial position to open the doorways to new and greater profits.

---

[13] Lawrence D. Miles, A Special American Machinist Report to the Metal Working Industries (New York: McGraw-Hill Book Co., Inc., 1949), p. 4.

index